QUILTING MASTERCLASS

    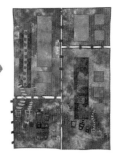

QUILTING
MASTERCLASS

◆

Inspirations and Techniques
from the Experts

KATHARINE GUERRIER

Martingale
& COMPANY

Bothell, Washington

A QUARTO BOOK

Martingale
& COMPANY

That
Patchwork
Place®

That Patchwork Place is an imprint of Martingale & Company

First published in 2000 by Martingale & Company
PO Box 118
Bothell, WA 98041-0118
www.patchwork.com

Library of Congress Cataloging-in-Publication data available.
ISBN 1-56477-327-2

QUAR.QMT

Conceived, designed,
and produced by
Quarto Publishing plc
The Old Brewery
6 Blundell Street
London N7 9BH

Editor Kate Michell
Art Editor Sally Bond
Assistant Art Director Penny Cobb
Text Editors Julie Brooke,
Sally MacEachern
Designer Liz Brown
Photographers Kevin Thomas
(Rockport, Massachusetts),
Colin Bowling (London, U.K.)
Illustrator Carrie Hill
Indexer Dorothy Frame

Art Director Moira Clinch
Publisher Piers Spence

Manufactured in China by Regent Publishing
Services, Ltd
Printed in China by Midas Printing Ltd

Contents

Above *Stylized birds and figures mingle with geometric motifs in The Greek Quilt by Sheena Norquay. A number of techniques were successfully combined to create this impressive and engaging quilt, which was inspired by the art of ancient Greece.*

INTRODUCTION

NEW DIRECTIONS

The current revival of interest in quilt-making began in the last quarter of the twentieth century and heralded a new approach to this traditional craft. In 1971, an exhibition at the Whitney Museum of American Art in New York, *Abstract Design in American Quilts*, made the groundbreaking point that quilts ought to be considered as a major influence in contemporary abstract art, and, finally, they were formally recognized as more than merely domestic bedcovers. Many makers embraced the new movement toward designing quilts purely as art for walls, while a painterly approach to the use of fabric and thread attracted artists to use the quilt form as their preferred medium. There can be no doubt that the Art Quilt is now firmly established and is internationally recognized as making an important contribution to the world of contemporary quiltmaking.

MASTERCLASS QUILTS

Gathering 50 contemporary quilts that could be deemed worthy of the term "Masterclass" was a huge challenge—the very term implied that each quilt had to demonstrate a high level of skill, combine originality and flair, and have the potential to influence and inspire others.

Both traditional and innovative techniques, along with the visions of the quiltmakers, were considered. Approaches varied enormously, but a common element ran through each artist's statement—enthusiasm and dedication toward their work.

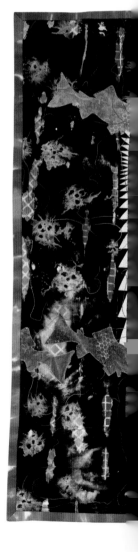

It also became clear that the commitment to pursuing quilting as a way of conveying personal ideas stems from many motives. Expressing pure enjoyment in the qualities and challenges of the medium resulted in abstractions such as Caryl Bryer Fallert's *Midnight Fantasy* and Friederike Kohlhaußen's *"Bruch" Folded 9*, while the need to deliver a warning produced Marta Amundson's *Tea for Trout = Trout for Tea*.

A wonderful mixture of expertise and wit appears in abundance, as in *Slip One, Knit One* by Sandie Lush, which

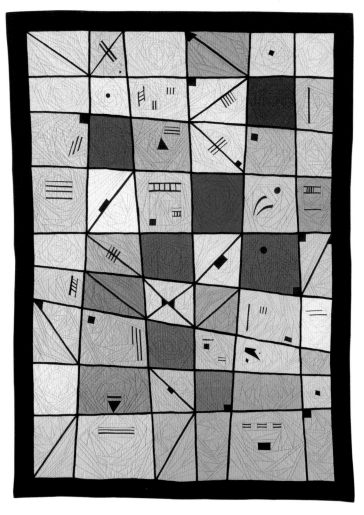

Above Dixie Haywood was moved to create this quilt after studying a small drawing by Vasily Kandinsky. She matched the colors and composition of the original painting, and then combined these elements with her own techniques to interpret and develop her source of inspiration.

Below Marta Amundson's *Tea for Trout = Trout for Tea* illustrates a plea for responsible policies toward the environment and the plight of endangered species.

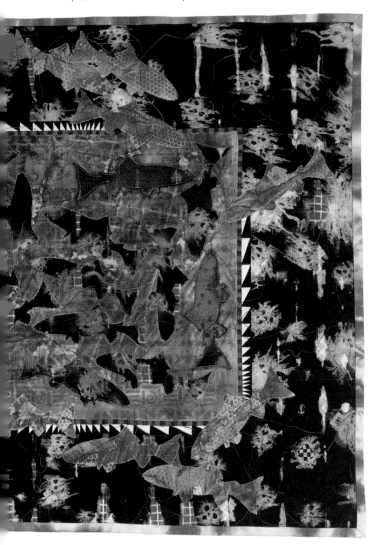

links the traditional skills of hand quilting and knitting in a contemporary "knitted" wallhanging, and in *Seven Quilts* by Sheila Yale, which gives an impression of quilts piled in layers, showing a striking mix of pattern and color.

The study of other artists' work is often a starting point for creative efforts, whether drawn from the fine art world, as in Dixie Haywood's homage to Kandinsky, *Soho Sunday*, or the decorative arts, as in Margaret Davidson's *Period Flair*—based on Art Deco watchstraps—and Sheena Norquay's *The Greek Quilt*, inspired by classic Greek vases. Each piece takes the spirit of the original and develops it into a unique work of art.

THE TECHNIQUES—UNITING TRADITION AND INNOVATION

Quiltmaking embraces a variety of different skills, and no one quilter is an expert in every aspect of the craft. This means that quilters, in the study of each other's work and the dialogue between them, learn continually, generating ideas and innovations, whether these are technique-driven or concerned with illustrating or interpreting themes.

Although my personal trademark as a quiltmaker is to develop traditional pieced block patterns into abstract quilts, my interest in other techniques was stimulated during the production of this book, and I felt compelled to try out some of the methods employed by others. Edwina Mackinnon's *Indigo Squares* inspired me to try fabric blooming, and I had great fun experimenting with simple printing on fabric using found objects such as leaves, coiled string, and bent card after working on Marta Amundson's *Tea for Trout = Trout for Tea*.

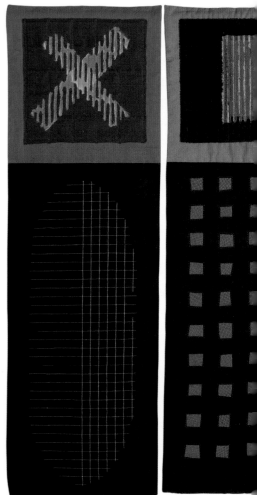

Above Similarities and differences, and the balances between them, are explored in Charlotte Yde's five-part quilt. Innovative techniques in a limited color palette were used in abstract symbolic images.

Left A perfect balance of composition, color, and skill is evident in Judy Mathieson's contemporary rendering of the traditional Mariner's Compass design.

In many cases, the limitations of a technique do not seem to hamper the accomplishment of an ideal. Judy Mathieson's *Bristol Stars*—which takes a contemporary tack on the traditional Mariner's Compass design—and Judy Dale's *Fantasy Form #6117* both demonstrate how far the use of a needle and thread can be taken thanks to the skill of their users.

Many of the featured artists have become well-known for establishing an innovative style that, in turn, influences the work of others. Katie Pasquini Masopust, with her "fractured" approach, creates new interpretations of realism, as demonstrated in *Glass Carafes*; Roberta Horton has drawn our attention to the qualities inherent in fabric types, as seen with *In Celebration*, which shows that in order to showcase special fabrics classic simplicity is sometimes best; and Diana Bunnell's *Black Minus Black* makes use of materials not usually associated with textiles, by being boldly printed with paint, adding further detail to a dynamic, abstract composition.

IN CONCLUSION

The work of contemporary quiltmakers is celebrated in exhibitions, books, and magazines the world over, and I hope that whether as a quiltmaker or as one who appreciates the decorative arts, the reader will find this particular collection exciting and inspiring. The diversity of color, skill, and vision demonstrates the phenomenal opportunities that quiltmaking presents, from the initial planning to the final stitch. Charlotte Yde, maker of *Kindred Spirits 1-5*, sums it up in her comment, "There is always a new challenge in the process of making quilts, and it is always a special feeling to have the visible, finished product in my hands." Quilters the world over will appreciate this sentiment, and it is to them that this book is dedicated.

TRADITION AND BEYOND

QUILTS MADE BY PREVIOUS GENERATIONS PROVIDE FIBER ARTISTS WITH A HERITAGE THAT CAN INFLUENCE AND INSPIRE. A STUDY OF ANTIQUE QUILTS IN MUSEUMS AND ART GALLERIES REVEALS THE RANGE OF SKILLS PUT TO USE IN THE CREATION OF THESE HEIRLOOMS. CONTEMPORARY QUILTMAKERS SHOW US THAT THESE SKILLS ARE STILL ALIVE, BY DRAWING ON TRADITIONS WHILE CHALLENGING AND REDEFINING THEM. THE QUILTS IN THIS CHAPTER PROVE THAT THE LEGACY OF ANTIQUE QUILTS IS A STRONG FOUNDATION ON WHICH TO BUILD AND DEVELOP NEW DIRECTIONS IN A LIVING CRAFT.

TROPICAL NINE PATCH

"Since I discovered quiltmaking I have made nearly 200 quilts and I have ideas (and certainly enough fabric) for many more. My first quilts were based on traditional patterns, and the work I am doing now still has its roots in tradition. Although I work full-time, I consider quilting as my second career. I took part in a basic color class with Michael James where we investigated high contrast: extreme light (almost white) fabrics against extreme dark (almost black) ones. I set out to make a quilt that would exploit these ideas but also use color to offset the high contrast blocks."

NANCY BRELAND

Nancy chose one of the most basic of traditional quilt patterns—the Nine Patch—to stretch her appreciation of extreme value contrast. As a foil for this regular, checkerboard grid effect, squares cut from batik fabrics were arranged into organized splashes of color, introducing movement into what would otherwise be a simple geometric design. The bright background blocks appear to float behind the strong grid formed by the dark, on-point squares. Rayon threads quilted in free-motion feather and flower motifs add texture and offset the regular geometry of the pieced design.

Overall design

Setting the Nine Patch blocks on point and separating them with the larger, background squares creates an impression of lightness. Inner and outer borders with corner squares frame the composition.

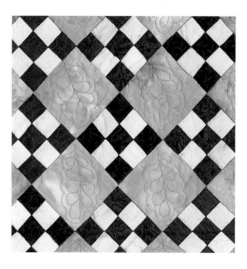

Range of fabrics

An extended range of extreme values— very dark and very light—was needed to make each Nine Patch block in a different set of fabrics. The very light fabrics were difficult to find.

Quilting

After securing the three layers of the quilt with straight stitching "in the ditch" (along the seams), free-motion feather motifs were worked in the larger squares.

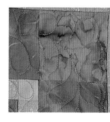

Borders and corner squares

Corner squares break the continuity of the inner and outer borders, echoing the squares in the blocks. The inner border fabric is used again in the binding.

Alternate blocks

The batik fabric chosen for the alternate blocks has, when carefully positioned, enough variety in its colors and design to provide effective splashes of color.

SIZE: 41 x 54 INCHES (104 x 137 CM)

ONE(1) NINE(9) ON NINE(9) NINES(9)—1999

"Since attending my first lesson I have been a keen patchworker. I enjoy patchwork and quilting, as they are crafts that allow one to be creative and practical at the same time. Although I have made 'art quilts,' I find that I am more drawn to traditional-format quilts that have been given a modern twist or interpretation. I particularly enjoy the illusions it is possible to create using color within patchwork, and I like the challenge of attempting to achieve them. All these aspects are, I suppose, a reflection of the fact that math was my favorite subject at school."

REBECCA COLLINS

This quilt was made for a Red and White challenge set by The Quilters' Guild. Given that red and white is a traditional color combination, Rebecca decided to reflect this by using basic Nine Patch blocks. The blocks and setting were drawn onto graph paper, then a single Nine Patch block on a much larger scale was drawn over the top of the original blocks, but slightly offset to create the illusion of transparency. Three different shades of red fabric were used on both the large and small Nine Patch blocks and where they overlapped. The border was treated in the same manner—a row of squares with another row overlapping and slightly offset. This witty reworking of the humble Nine Patch has elevated it to new heights of sophistication.

Overall design

The large and small Nine Patch blocks and the pieced borders are effectively "floated" by the plain white blocks that separate and surround them, giving a lightness of touch to the overall design. Elaborate quilting decorates the white areas and influences the shaped edges of the quilt. The three red fabrics used in the quilt top were repeated in the binding to give a final flourish to this exuberant quilt.

Preparation

To ensure that the blocks and the border were in proportion to each other and the white background, Rebecca's first step was to create a scale drawing of the quilt on graph paper.

Transparency

The illusion of transparency is created by the subtle color change from light to deep red where the large and small blocks overlap.

Size: 43½ x 45 inches (110 x 114 cm)

Quilting

The quilting on the blocks reflects the two different scales. Decorative quilting in an original feather pattern was worked over the plain areas and borders.

Binding

The piped edge of the red binding creates a bold frame, and serves to make a final statement.

Piecing

The quilt was pieced by machine—tiny squares and narrow rectangles were necessary to achieve the overlapping effect.

OPEN GATE

"My favorite expression is, 'I feel a quilt coming on!' I just can't help getting started once I've found fabrics appropriate to my needs. I was not originally someone who did needlework—I trained as a physical education teacher, but I saw my first quilt 15 years ago and just had to make one like it. I learned the hard way, through tradition first and then found I had some creativity, which I may never have discovered but for patchwork. I specifically enjoy hand reverse appliqué and color."

DILYS FRONKS

This quilt is a real showstopper, with its skillfully blended colors and elaborately worked wrought iron gate. The design was fabric led, put together on a vertical design wall. The technique of blending the colors together like this is often referred to as watercolor or colorwash. The fabric squares, which measure 2½ inches (6.5 cm), were fitted together rather like a jigsaw, and pictures developed spontaneously. When the position of each square had been decided, the squares were sewn together in strips, and the strips stitched into rows to produce a gentle transition between values and colors. The gateway, borders, and foliage detail were created with reverse appliqué.

Overall design

Although the "garden" is composed of pieced squares of fabric, the squares are so cleverly blended into flowerbeds, paths, hedges, and sky we can almost believe it a pictorial representation. The black image superimposed on this background defines the colors, giving them a greater luminescence and perspective.

Colorwash or watercolor squares

This technique of blending colors rather than exploiting contrasting values was pioneered by Deirdre Amsden.

The overlay

The appliqué technique Dilys used presents many technical difficulties. The evenness and symmetry of the narrow strips and the curves of the gate required great patience.

REVERSE APPLIQUÉ

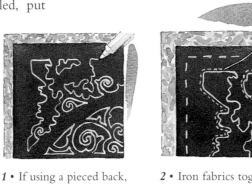

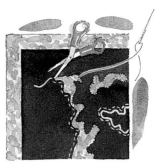

1 • If using a pieced back, prepare this first. Alternatively, reverse appliqué can be done using one piece of plain or printed fabric for the bottom layer. Transfer the design to the right side of the top fabric using a lightbox and a fabric marker.

2 • Iron fabrics together, right sides uppermost. Baste around the appliqué design close to the marked lines.

3 • Cut a ½ inch (1.5 cm) long segment of the top layer, leaving a ¼ inch (0.75 cm) seam allowance. Stitch the layers together, matching the thread to the top fabric. Continue working in ½ inch (1.5 cm) segments. Clip into tight bends and corners, grouping stitches closer together to prevent fraying. Use the needle to turn under the raw edges just ahead of the stitching.

PINWHEEL MAZE

"This quilt is my attempt to interpret the patterns used within the quiltmaking tradition and develop them into an original design. I study the geometric patterns of pieced quilts, often drawing from more than one design to contribute to a piece of work. My color choices are purely intuitive—I work mainly with commercially available patterned fabrics, using many in one quilt, trying to harmonize, blend, and contrast the colors and tones to achieve the results I am aiming for."

KATHARINE GUERRIER

Quilting

Quilting adds an extra dimension to a quilt by creating surface texture. Here, straight-line machine quilting in variegated threads follows the patterns within the blocks.

Working method

The composition of the quilt was devised by arranging blocks on a large pinboard, and then rearranging them to reach a final design decision.

Although at first glance this quilt has a contemporary look, Katharine developed the design by studying traditional American quilts. The constraints imposed on early quiltmakers by a shortage of fabrics meant that quilt patterns often employed dark/light contrast within the blocks. Katharine's quilt is an attempt to interpret patterns used within this tradition and develop them into new designs. *Pinwheel Maze* uses the strategy of contrasting value placement in conjunction with a novel piecing method. Pinwheel blocks were made from harmonizing fabrics, then wedge-shaped sections were cut from the edges. This quilt is part of the revival of interest in quiltmaking, in which the allure of color, pattern, and texture has superseded our ancestors' more practical motives for making quilts, while paying homage to their achievements.

Overall design

The Pinwheel blocks were set into squares, half dark and half light with a diagonal division—an influence of the traditional Log Cabin block design. The maze was created by arranging the blocks so that the dark and light areas in the quilt form paths and diamonds across its surface. Techniques used in the making of this quilt were also essentially modern—rotary cutting, quick piecing, and machine quilting.

Inspiration

Each Log Cabin block is divided equally into dark and light sides, offering a wealth of design opportunities and setting options.

Size: 60 x 70 inches (152 x 178 cm)

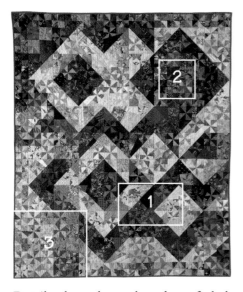

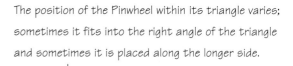

The position of the Pinwheel within its triangle varies; sometimes it fits into the right angle of the triangle and sometimes it is placed along the longer side.

Detail 1: Dark/light block

Pinwheels are made more visible by the use of some bright fabrics that contrast with the triangles surrounding them.

Details show how the play of dark against light influenced the quilt. The dark/light block clearly defines the diagonal lines so important to the composition. The machine quilting is visible across both parts. In the large, dark diamond, the alternate block extends the dark area, resulting in a jewel-like richness. At the bottom left-hand side of the quilt, the alternate blocks are made from light fabrics to balance the composition.

Each side of the main blocks contains a cropped Pinwheel surrounded by fabrics chosen from the dark or light set.

Pinwheels for the dark side consist of a dark fabric with a medium or bright one, and for the light side a light fabric with a medium or bright combination.

Detail 2: The alternate block

The alternate block is constructed slightly differently. Pinwheels are made and trimmed in the same way, but there are four to each block, and fabrics from the same set are used in each block—all dark or all light.

Color study

The color references came from a collection of patterned fabrics, and the choice and combinations used were purely a result of Katharine's intuitive feel for color and pattern. The selected fabrics were then built together to achieve the desired effect. The effects of value—light against dark—are more important than color in such a quilt.

The all-dark and all-light Pinwheels can be used to extend the dark and light areas. This is how the large, dark diamond was created.

MAKING AND TRIMMING THE PINWHEELS

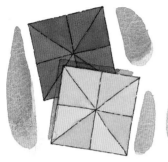 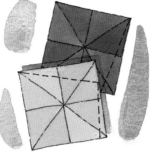 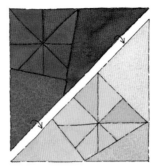 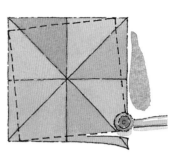

1 • Two trimmed Pinwheels are required for each block, one for each side. Vary the size of the Pinwheels, but make one measuring 5 inches (12.7 cm) square as a starting point.

2 • Once the Pinwheels have been made and pressed, trim each one differently—this gives each block variety and movement. If the Pinwheel is to be positioned in the right angle of the block, maintain a 90 degree angle in one corner.

3 • Sew fabric pieces to the Pinwheels and trim to make two triangles as shown. Join the triangles to make a block.

4 • For filler blocks, make the Pinwheels slightly larger and then trim them as shown.

Detail 3: Pieced binding & alternate blocks

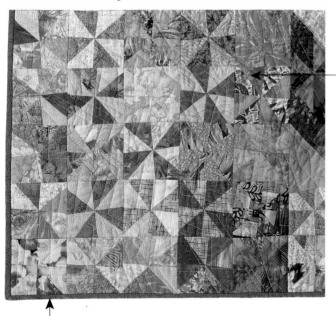

Alternate blocks are positioned in the lower left-hand corner of the quilt, moving from a darker area into a medium light one to balance the composition.

5 • Join four trimmed Pinwheels to make a colorful filler block.

The binding on a quilt provides an opportunity to make a final statement. Here, short red inserts in the mid-blue binding are set at random distances and provide focus points along the edges of the quilt.

IN CELEBRATION

"The fabrics in this quilt were chosen for the glory of their patterns and the variety of techniques used to produce them. Some of these fabrics are very finely engineered, others are seemingly done freehand. I enjoy this contrast—rigid versus casual. African hand-dyed and tie-dyed fabrics, silk-screened examples from Zimbambwe, and American hand-dyed painted and silk-screened cloth, all form a quickly composed collection of fabrics."

ROBERTA HORTON

Roberta has written several books which throw new light on existing traditions, and she has inspired fresh interest in fabrics that quilters may originally have discarded as being unsuitable. Categories such as plaids and stripes, and Japanese and African fabrics have all received her attention. The quilt illustrated here, *In Celebration*, is just that—a showcase for a number of fabrics that inspired Roberta to explore and understand how the fabric is built. To this end, the quilt was constructed from simple shapes that were assembled in three vertical strips. Working directly with the fabrics on a design wall, the quilt was composed of irregular-sized rectangles, finely balanced to give maximum visual impact to each fabric. The inclusion of Pinwheels in each of the main sections adds focus points, leading the eye across and into other areas of the quilt to explore the visual complexity of the fabrics.

Overall design

Each of the three vertical columns of fabric is composed of a collage of rectangles interspersed with Pinwheels. The columns are separated by borders of a black fabric with large circular motifs. The outer border displays a collection of textured fabrics in earth tones that reflect the main color palette.

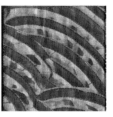

Quilting

Quilting, done by hand and machine with some sashiko stitching, was dictated by the fabric patterns.

Pinwheels

The Pinwheels introduce a change of direction, as the diagonal lines create movement and interest.

Sashiko stitching

Sashiko stitching is a traditional Japanese quilting technique. A thick thread is used and the stitches are longer than regular quilting stitches. Traditionally, sashiko follows geometric designs of varying complexity. A strong color contrast is used between the thread and the fabric.

SASHIKO QUILTING

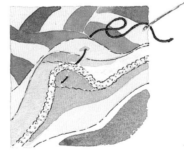

1 • Thread a large-eyed needle with a length of coton à broder or perle cotton No. 5 or No. 8. Tie a knot at the end of the thread and pull it though the fabric so that it is hidden in the middle of the quilt.

2 • Sashiko is a simple running stitch. Concentrate on sewing three or four stitches to the inch (2.5 cm) Work along marked lines or the fabric design. Secure completed lines by darning the thread ends into the quilt's inner layer.

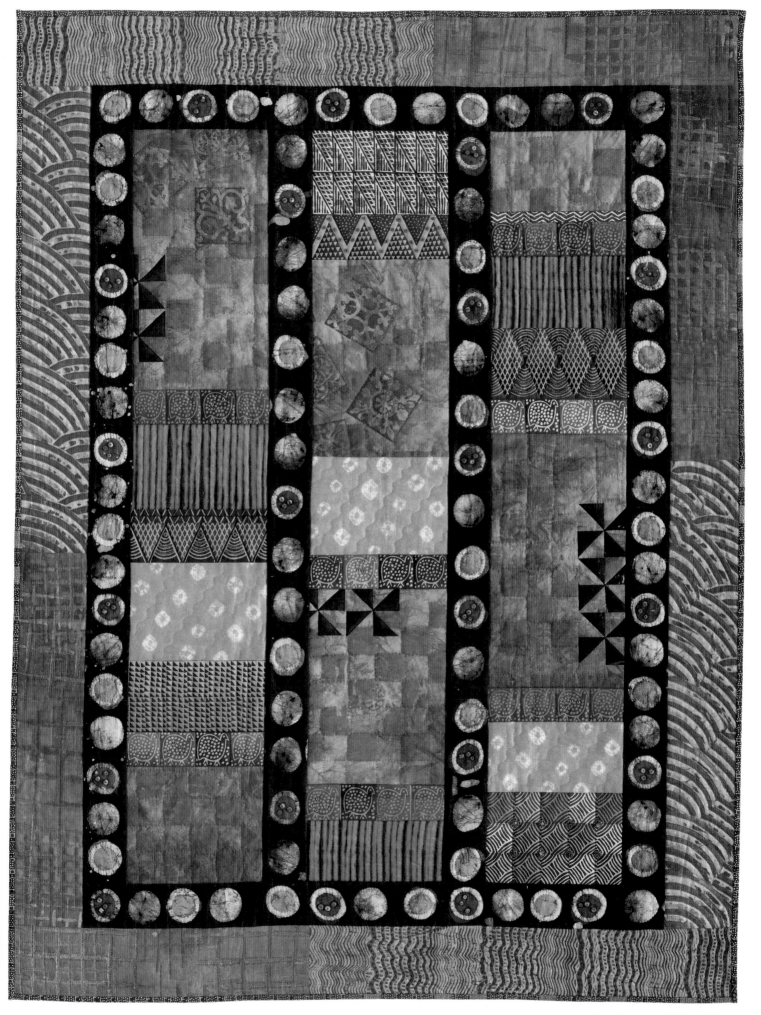

Size: 40 x 54 inches (102 x 137 cm)

TIDEMARK, CAPE TRIBULATION

"Like the majority of my quilts, Tidemark is inspired by the Australian landscape. This one recreates a photograph I took on the beach at Cape Tribulation in Northern Queensland, where the rain forest overhangs the beach. Along with the usual shells and seaweed, the tidemark contained a crazy jumble of leaves, twigs, and seedpods. Crazy patchwork seemed the ideal manner in which to interpret the juxtaposition of forest litter washed into the sea and then swept back onto the beach with the returning tide. It also allowed me the indulgence of playing with traditional hand embroidered crazy patchwork while producing a contemporary quilt."

WENDY LUGG

When designing the quilt Wendy went straight from photo to fabrics. Two of the fabrics in particular suited sand imagery, and these became the key fabrics around which the others were built. The leaf images were printed directly using real leaves; others were printed with stencils. This quilt is part of a series of fragment quilts that developed in response to the simple but wonderful old textile fragment that Wendy has collected over the years and on her travels. Wendy felt it was important to use natural fibers, handwork, and large stitching in this contemporary piece, where the traditional genre of crazy patchwork is used effectively to interpret a love of the natural environment.

Overall design

An irregular shaped background, with the bottom edge cut away, is the foundation of the quilt, with crazy patchwork details spilling over the edges. Most of the appliquéd detail is concentrated at the top of the quilt, but the large-scale stipple quilting gives the quilt texture. A limited palette of light through medium beige colors emphasizes the theme of sand transformed by the sea.

Embroidery techniques

Crazy patchwork borrows techniques from embroidery. The random stipple quilting—worked here with big stitches and a blending thread—puckered the fabric to produce the look of ripples on sand.

Inspiration

Taken by Wendy, this photograph of debris left by the tide shows fine details and offers rich artistic inspiration.

SIZE: 28 X 36 INCHES
(72 X 92 CM)

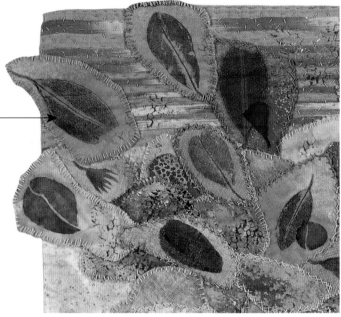

Freestanding appliqué leaves stray off the top edges of the quilt, adding a three-dimensional element. This detail complements and balances the shaped bottom of the quilt.

A combination of appliqué, embroidery, and quilting create a wealth of detail and texture on the surface of this quilt. Contemporary ideas, such as shaping the base, were used alongside the traditional embroidery stitches that appear in old crazy quilts.

Detail 2: Tidemark debris

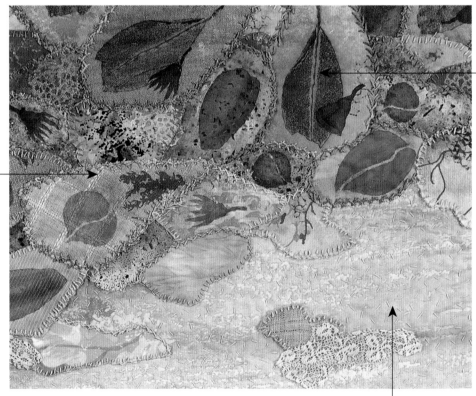

The appliqué shapes are surrounded by embroidery stitches that are both functional and decorative. They cover the raw edges of the pieces and fasten them to the background. A variety of linear stitches were used to link and embellish the shapes.

Seeding is a form of stitching in which short straight stitches are worked in random directions. In this piece, they form part of the quilting that fastens the three layers of the quilt together, puckering the fabric to give an impression of rippled sand.

Detail 3: Water's edge

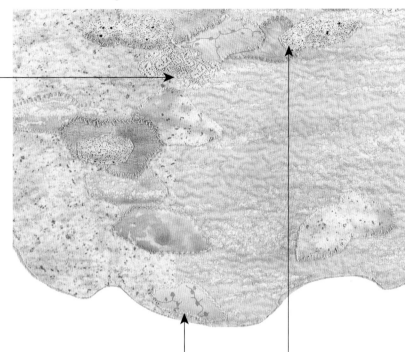

The relatively subdued color palette at the base of the quilt contrasts with the darker area at the top. The subtly shaded fabric is, in some areas, overprinted with images of leaves and other details and is complemented by the stitchery.

Realistic details of the tidemark were created by first overprinting onto the fabrics. By inking the backs of leaves and then pressing them onto the fabric, the lifelike texture of the leaf was transferred to the fabric. Further images of seedpods, twigs, and other detritus were stenciled onto the fabric.

The bottom of the quilt is shaped to reflect the tidemark theme, effectively expressing the quality of water over shifting sands.

In the lower section of the quilt, the pattern of retreating waves embossed in sand is conjured with a combination of quilting and collaged appliqué shapes.

EMBROIDERY STITCHES SUITABLE FOR CRAZY PATCHWORK

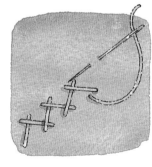

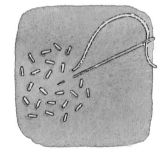

1 • Feather stitch Bring the needle out at the top center. Take small stitches alternately from the left and the right to the center, keeping the thread under the needle point to create the "feather" effect.

2 • Herringbone stitch Work the stitching from left to right. Bring the needle out at the lower line and insert on the upper line a little to the right, then take a small stitch to the left. Insert the needle on the lower line, a little to the right, and take a small stitch to the left. Keep the stitches even.

3 • Blanket stitch Work the stitching from left to right. Bring the thread out on the lower line, insert the needle in position in the upper line, and bring it out to the right on the lower line, pulling the thread over the first stitch. Repeat, keeping the stitches even.

4 • Seeding Make short, straight stitches of equal length at random over the surface of the fabric. To exert tension and produce a slightly puckered effect, pull the thread as you work.

SLIP ONE, KNIT ONE

*"The challenge of working within a theme—
the game of cricket—through the medium
of wholecloth quilts was a difficult one. I
considered aspects of the cricketing theme
that had stripes to link with the idea of the
traditional strippy quilt. Initially, I worked
around the idea of the mowed pitch. Then, I
hit on the idea of a cricket sweater. I set out to
recreate the look and texture as accurately as
possible. I think it is the actual size of the piece
that has surprised people who have only seen a
photograph—they all assumed it was life-size."*

SANDIE LUSH

Here, the wholecloth quilt is given an almost surreal quality because, although it resembles a sweater, it is the size of a bed quilt. The link that is established between the two traditional skills of hand knitting and wholecloth quilting entertains us with its wit and commands our admiration for its visual impact. The design was first drawn onto tracing paper in pencil. Then, when Sandie was happy with it, it was redrawn in black ink. The fabric was placed over the drawing and the design traced with a brown watercolor pencil. The fabric chosen was charmeuse polyester satin, to reflect the texture of the quilting. Wool batting and cotton backing were used and it was stitched by hand using a soft quilting thread. The outer edges of the quilt are bound, using a bias strip on the curves and mitering at the corners.

Three spools
Copyright prevented Sandie from reproducing the club's logo—the club's three lions usually appear at the base of the V-neck. To recognize their existence and continue the cricket and quilting link, Sandie created a logo of three spools of thread.

Label
The label detail was ingenious. Fabric care labels were found on the Internet and incorporated into a computer program. The label was then printed onto photo transfer paper and transferred onto a wide ribbon.

Overall design
The title of the exhibition—*Under the Covers*—was chosen to draw ideas from the world of quilts and the world of cricket, because the venue for the exhibition was to be Lord's cricket ground in London. Sandie linked the two by combining the wholecloth quilt with the shape of a traditional cricket sweater worn by the club's members. The quilting stitches reproduce the details of the knitting stitches perfectly, even as far as the lines of cable, the inside of the sweater, and the ribbed edging.

Quilting
Sandie deliberately varied the density of the quilting stitches so that the unquilted areas between the cables were thrown into high relief. The puffy quality of the wool wadding was also exploited to contribute to the effect. The inside of the sweater would be visible through the V-neck opening, so here the quilting stitches had to line up precisely to reproduce the appearance of knitted stitches seen from the wrong side. The graphic texture that can be created by quilting stitches alone is impressive.

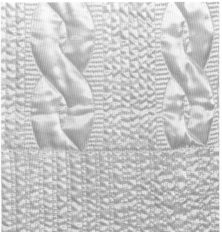

Surface texture

The graphic surface texture is created entirely by quilting stitches, demonstrating the skill and imagination that went into this piece of work. The sheen on the quilt is slightly reflective, enhancing the bas-relief quality created by the stitching.

Binding

Great attention to detail went into creating as realistic a "sweater" as possible—Sandie even went so far as to use bias binding for the curved edges and straight binding for the long edges, mitered at each corner.

MY HEART'S DELIGHT

"I attended a workshop with American quilter Moneca Calvert, one of whose specialties is to set heart shapes into quilts; so when Quilts U.K. made hearts their theme, I was inspired to create a piece of work for the show. One surprise that emerged after designing the quilt was the large star in the center. Because hearts are the strongest element in the quilt, and because it is my favorite piece of work, I decided to name the quilt 'My Heart's Delight.'"

MARY MAYNE

In quiltmaking, ideas and inspirations often come from the exchange of ideas between artists and makers. Mary's quilt, the result of meeting Moneca Calvert, was designed using simple circular shapes in a variety of sizes. Mary designed on paper, using objects such as wine glasses and thread spools to draw the circles, and thus continued a long-standing tradition of using everyday objects to make templates established by early quiltmakers. Being a symmetrical quilt, Mary was able to work from a full-size quarter-section paper pattern. The fabric pieces were hand stitched, and the curved seams proved technically difficult because Mary had to take care not to stretch the fabrics. A number of quilting designs were used—some traditional, and others designed expressly for this quilt. Combined with the harmonizing colors, this quilt is full of quiet power, which repays prolonged viewing.

Overall design

Mary chose cottons in lavender, blue, and white for this quilt. The elegant curved-feather motif in the white areas of the large hearts provides a focus for the eye, while the cross-hatching and echo quilting on the dark blue border add surface texture.

Piecing

Initially an attempt was made to machine stitch the pieces together, but this proved too difficult, and so the quilt was hand pieced, working from the center shapes toward the outside.

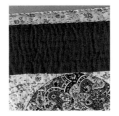

Binding

Mary bound her quilt by turning the backing fabric over to the right side and stitching it onto the front of the quilt. By using one of the quilt fabrics for the backing, Mary connected the edges to the central motifs.

Quilting

A close web of quilting creates additional suface texture on the quilt. Here the patchwork and quilting blend well, complementing each other beautifully. Quilting stitches are always more visible on plain fabric and add a decorative element to the work.

Contrast

A nicely balanced contrast of light, medium, and dark values between the fabrics shows off the heart motifs to best advantage, while the variety of scale in the patterned fabrics provides visual texture.

SIZE: 60 X 60 INCHES (152 X 152 CM)

KENKA

"The Kenka cherry blossom is one of the symbols of Tokyo county. I was asked to design a quilt with the theme of the county flower for an exhibition in Yokohama, so I put the cherry blossom in the center. The composition also includes ginkgo leaves and yurikamome birds—also symbols of the county. I designed the quilt using Stained Glass patchwork, and using a mixture of fabrics including cotton and brocade."

HIROMITSU TAKANO

In Japan there is a long tradition of decorative arts and crafts, and their practitioners are highly regarded. Hiromitsu's work has been featured in several publications and often appears in the Japanese magazine *Patchwork Quilt Tsushin*. He also appears on national television demonstrating arts and crafts. His quilts have been exhibited both at home in Japan and abroad. In *Kenka* a balance is struck between technique and artistry. The quilt was made using a form of appliqué called Stained Glass, which characterizes quilts by bold patterns and brilliant colors. Areas of color were separated by fabric "leading," so it was important to create a design without too many small or intricate shapes. All the pieces of fabric for the different sections of the quilt were cut and assembled onto a large backing fabric, rather like a jigsaw puzzle.

Overall design

A formal design of flowers, leaves, and birds is contained by the linear tracery of the surrounding bold blue and rust-colored strips. The large, central cherry blossom is the dominant motif, while the 16 birds hidden in the outer section must be searched out by the viewer. Japanese fabrics are noted for their fine colors and quality, and here the choices admirably match the quilt's themes.

Central cherry blossom motif

The large petals of the cherry blossom are composed of a number of different fabrics, pieced together before they are positioned in the center of the quilt. This separates each petal into sections, adding interest and visual texture. Bold strips of rust-colored fabric are used to provide definition for the stamens and around the petals.

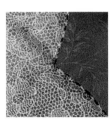

Color

The decorative circle and terra-cotta background complement the dominant pink, blue, and green fabrics.

"Leading" strips

The "leading"—
fabric strips that
separate areas of
the design—had to
be cut on the bias
to make them
curve around the
shapes. They were
stitched carefully
by hand, covering
the raw edges
of the patches
and linking the
design elements.

Birds

Finding the 16
yurikamome birds
that are hidden in
the outer sections
of the quilt is
quite a puzzle.
Once found, they
emphasize the
symmetry of
the composition.

Size: 24 x 24 inches (61 x 61 cm)

THE GOOD TIMES

"I came across quiltmaking when I lived in the U.S. I took a course in basic techniques and became hooked. At last I had found a means of self expression! It was an opportunity to escape into the kaleidoscopic world of color that had always fascinated me. The main motivation for making this quilt was a challenge to recycle a bag of exotic fabrics. I feel very conscious of our throwaway society, and as the millennium approached I wanted to revive the old values of thrift and economy and I was determined not to buy yet more fabrics."

CAROLINE WILKINSON

Caroline chose the Crazy Quilt style for her blocks because it was in keeping with her fabrics, which came from a bag of scraps from an upmarket dressmaker, a free bag of top quality furnishing samples, together with a collection of carefully hoarded scraps of silk, satin, taffeta, velvet, ribbon, and metallics. Influences were also drawn from the traditional classic Log Cabin Barn Raising. The Log Cabin is known for its versatile exploitation of contrasting dark and light fabrics, thereby making it an ideal vehicle for a scrap quilt. The quilt blocks were constructed on foundation squares using the Log Cabin method. Before assembling the blocks into the quilt, they were embellished with braids or machine embroidery using decorative threads.

Overall design

The overall design of radiating dark and light diamonds is a clever combination of the Crazy Quilt and Log Cabin Barn Raising patterns. To achieve this effect, the blocks are set on point. Fragments of other classic block patterns, such as the Nine Patch and Fan, also appear in individual blocks.

Inspiration

The rich, luminescent colors of stained glass windows were one of the color references Caroline drew on for inspiration when making *The Good Times*.

Working methods

Caroline seldom designs on paper, instead she works directly with fabrics on a vertical design wall. She takes photographs with an instant camera to back up decisions about the overall design.

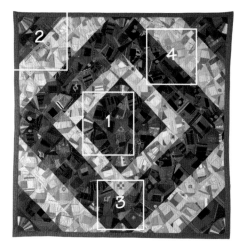

Although each block is made up of a unique arrangement of fabric shapes, the overall structure of the design is dictated by the arrangement of diamonds in alternating dark and light fabrics. Fan motifs were used in some of the corner blocks—this was a popular pattern in early Crazy Quilts.

Detail 1: Quilt center

The center part of the quilt consists of 16 blocks, all made using dark fabrics. The blocks are set on point—changing the large square into a diamond.

Some corner blocks have a fan motif, the outlines of which are embellished with linear embroidery stitches.

Additional interest is provided by the variety of shapes and patch sizes in each block.

Detail 2: Mixing exotic fabrics

These Log Cabin blocks were made on a square of foundation fabric. A foundation stabilizes fabrics that might ordinarily be unsuitable for patchwork and makes it possible to mix different weights of fabric. The stabilizing nature of the foundation also makes it possible to ignore grain line when placing fabrics.

Colors were graded through the diamonds. Warm and cool tones were clustered together within the constraints of the dark and light fabric groups.

Contrasting values, rather than color, establish the design lines when using the principles of the Log Cabin method.

Detail 3: Recycled blocks

The inclusion in the quilt of fragments of blocks left over from previous projects—like the Nine Patch block seen here—continues the underlying theme of recycling.

Machine embroidery with decorative threads, braids, and ribbons embellish the blocks in the tradition of nineteenth-century Crazy Quilts.

Detail 4: Batting

Rather than quilting, Caroline tacked the top, batting, and backing together with embroidery thread in a variety of colors; this created a sculptured surface.

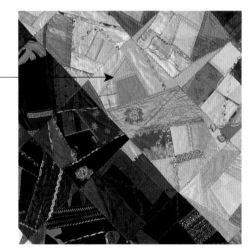

CRAZY LOG CABIN CONSTRUCTION

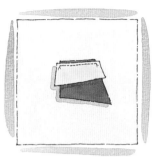

1 • Place the center patch of the Log Cabin on a square of lightweight foundation fabric, such as muslin.

2 • With right sides together, align the second piece with one edge of the center patch. Stitch through all three layers.

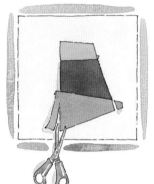

3 • Flip the second piece over and press it flat. Trim the sides of the second piece even with the first. Continue adding patches until the foundation is covered.

4 • Square up the block and stitch ⅛ inch (0.3 cm) from each edge to secure. When joining blocks, sew through all layers and press seams open to reduce bulk.

Color study

Caroline made a collection of pictures to use as color references—mosaic floor tiles, colorful ceramics, sunset colors, and contemporary quilts. She then chose exotic fabrics, including silk, satin, and taffeta, to reflect the qualities of color and light that she found in these various sources.

ILLUSION: TWO DIMENSIONS INTO THREE

◆

Through the manipulation of shape and color, quiltmakers create impressions of depth, distance, and movement, crafting an illusion of three dimensions on the flat surface of a quilt. Fabric artists challenge themselves to accomplish ever more sophisticated illusions, creating fabulous effects of transparency and perspective. This chapter illustrates stunning applications of dimensional illusion in a group of quilts that presents us with far more than initially meets the eye.

MIDNIGHT FANTASY

"I love the tactile qualities of cloth and the unlimited color range made possible by hand dyeing and painting. For as long as I can remember I have expressed myself through art. My formal training was in design, drawing, and studio painting. After many years of painting, sewing, and experimenting with other media, I discovered that fabric was the artistic medium that best expressed my personal vision. The focus of my work is on the qualities of color, line, and texture that will engage the emotions of the viewer, evoking a sense of mystery, excitement, or joy."

CARYL BRYER FALLERT

Caryl Bryer Fallert, internationally recognized for her award-winning art quilts, creates illusions of movement, depth, and luminosity in her quilts. For this design, the large, swirling shapes were drawn full size onto a four-foot square (0.4-square meter) piece of paper. From this, templates were made for the individual pieces of fabric for the quilt. Curved-seam piecing presented more of a challenge than the usual straight seams, and the spiky black and white curves had to be pieced on paper foundations before being incorporated into the main design. Many different threads and a number of machine-quilting patterns were used. This piece is a fine example of Caryl's attention to detail, which has earned her a reputation for meticulous craftsmanship and stunning design.

Inspiration

Inspiration for this quilt came during a sleepless night when Caryl made a series of small drawings to pass the time. One of these drawings was later refined to create the design for the quilt.

Foundation piecing

Piecing on paper foundations made it possible to incorporate tiny bits of fabric into the pieced design with accuracy.

Overall design

Although this piece of work is abstract, it was nevertheless inspired by visual impressions collected in Caryl's travels and everyday life. She states that her work is about seeing, experiencing, and imagining, rather than a pictorial representation of any specific object or species. Here, changing perspectives create an illusion of three-dimensional depth.

SIZE: 48 X 48 INCHES (122 X 122 CM)

By painting and dyeing her own fabric, Caryl increased the possible color options and degrees of shading and transparency, which add to the three-dimensional illusion. The composition of curved shapes and the heavily textured quilting also increased the dimensional impact of Caryl's work.

Detail 1: Optical illusions

The illusion of movement, depth, and luminosity are common to most of Caryl's quilts, as she likes to focus on exploring the quality of color, line, and texture.

Where one shape crosses over another, the effect of transparency is achieved by the clever use of color at the crossover point.

Detail 2: Quilting

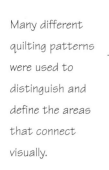
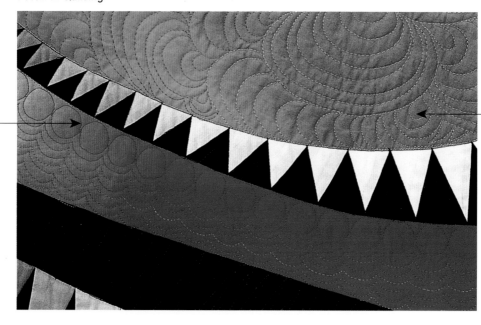

Many different quilting patterns were used to distinguish and define the areas that connect visually.

The heavily quilted surface displays both free-motion and regular machine quilting.

Detail 3: Binding

Detail 4: Precision piecing

The pieced black and white triangles in their curving paths cleverly give an effect of perspective by altered angles and gradually increasing lengths.

Tiny pieces, sharp points, and asymmetrical shapes that would be difficult to piece using traditional methods fit together perfectly thanks to paper foundation piecing.

The black used for the binding and the sharply pointed zigzag shapes complements the bright colors, giving them additional impact. The binding echoes, and sometimes merges with, the dark areas of the quilt to contain the composition.

FOUNDATION PIECING

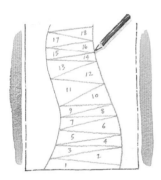

1 • Draw your design on a paper foundation, allowing at least ¼ inch (0.75 cm) on all edges for joining the pieced panel to adjacent fabrics. Establish the order of piecing and number the design.

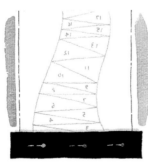

2 • Place fabric patch 1 right-side up over area 1 on the blank side of the paper foundation. Make sure it is big enough to cover the area it is designed for.

3 • Lay patch 2 on patch 1, right sides together, and flip patch 2 up to make sure it covers the desired area. Turn patch 2 back down, pin, turn the paper over, and stitch on the line between areas 1 and 2. Turn the paper over, trim the excess fabric, leaving a ¼ inch (0.75 cm) seam allowance, then flip patch 2 over to lie flat on the foundation.

4 • Repeat step 3 until the foundation is covered and the panel completed. Remove the paper from the back of the panel.

NOT A CALICO CHICKEN, FANTASY FORM #6117

"This quilt is the fourth in a series of 'fantasy form' quilts, all of which evolve from original drawings or doodles. The abstract curved designs are usually drawn when I am occupied with other things—this one was doodled when I was on the phone. I figure I was born to be a quilter, having the eclectic and diverse talents that quilting requires: an eye for color, a passion for fabric, sewing skills, and a lot of persistence! The title of the quilt refers to my dedication to the quilt as an art form, and my determination not to succumb to the temptation to make small, inexpensive items to support myself."

JUDY B. DALES

To begin constructing this quilt, a full-size pattern had to be drawn—Judy used an overhead projector to help her. The pattern was refined and each piece was carefully labeled with details. Cardboard templates were made, and each piece of fabric was cut out individually. Before the pieces of fabric were stitched together, some of the background pieces were embellished with tulle and chiffon. Judy machine quilted with rayon thread that matched the color of the fabrics. In the days of rotary-cut and quick-pieced quilts, it is impressive to find a quilter who prefers to use traditional techniques (using templates and cutting individual fabric pieces), but this is the only way such a complex quilt could be made.

Overall design

An intricate arrangement of undulating curved shapes in harmonious colors—pinks, purples, and turquoise—is set over a pale background. The main lines of the design are emphasized by a rich, dark blue fabric, which swirls organically through the composition. Quilting lines echo and complement the forms. Judy's dedication to her ideal shows in the meticulous execution of the quilt, in which the spirit of the design has not been sacrificed to the challenges of construction.

Quilting

Free-form quilting covers the surface, and extra design motifs add to the overall impact of the quilt. Close quilting stitches add surface texture, increasing the tactile quality of the piece.

Marbled fabrics

This quilt was a collaboration between Judy and textile artist Marjorie Lee Bevis. Marjorie, who creates fabrics with an abstract surface design similar to marbled paper, asked Judy to make a quilt using examples of her work.

Background

Subtle blends of pale fabrics were chosen for the background. Extra layers of sheer fabrics—to enrich the design, soften the edges, and create a water-color effect—were added to some of the background pieces before the top was stitched.

Size: 61 x 47 inches (155 x 119 cm)

Curved shapes

The composition of curving shapes was so intricate that each piece needed its own template. They all had to fit smoothly together, presenting the maker with many challenges: deciding on the fabrics and colors, devising an order of construction, and managing the construction itself.

NOT A CALICO CHICKEN, FANTASY FORM #6117 **45**

PERIOD FLAIR

"I studied art and block printing, which led me to develop a strong geometric design style for my quilts. I made my first quilt 20 years ago and I started with traditional block designs. I am interested in architecture and art deco designs, which have influenced my work for the last ten years. A recurring feature of my design style is the use of solid colored fabrics. This began from my love of Amish quilts, but I think it also serves to heighten the effect of the quilting stitches."

MARGARET DAVIDSON

Margaret has used the traditional methods of hand piecing and hand quilting. The linear qualities of art deco designs led Margaret to develop the quilt as a "strippy"—that is, the geometric patterns are organized as long strips running the length of the quilt, rather than as repeated square blocks. Before beginning to stitch, Margaret drew the design on graph paper to scale, then considered the placement of the different colors. These were influenced in some part by the quantities of fabric available. When all the design decisions were made, Margaret made a template for each shape in the quilt. The broad central column is flanked on each side by narrower ones. Each strip is composed of a different design sequence. As a foil to the straight-line geometry of the patches, quilted ovals and circles create additional texture.

Overall design

Although the overall design follows the formula of the traditional "strippy" quilt, the link with tradition is tenuous. The strips are of different widths and each presents a column of varied geometric shapes in rhythmic complexities. There is an evident dialogue between the clear colors and the striking design. The mitered corners and the change from dark to light values in the border strips create three-dimensional illusions.

Inspiration

Margaret loves to introduce her passion for modern art and architecture into her quilting. On this occasion, she studied art deco watchstraps.

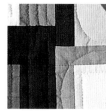

Complementary angles

The inclusion of diagonal, as well as horizontal and vertical lines, gives the design movement and emphasizes its links with the art deco movement.

Visual texture

Although the colors are solid, there is a slight sueded texture to the surface of the fabrics as a result of the dyeing technique.

Hand piecing

Although it was time-consuming, Margaret chose to hand piece her quilt top in order to accurately match up the different segments.

SIZE: 70 X 80 INCHES (178 X 203 CM)

SIXTY DEGREES AND FALLING

"I have sewn all my life. I made my first quilt—a hand appliquéd baby quilt for a friend—when I was in high school. I estimate that over the last 30 years I have made more than a thousand quilts, and at least one third of those are bed quilts. The aspect of quiltmaking that I most enjoy is designing my own quilts. I have turned to machine quilting to speed up production and make all the quilts I've imagined, although I do enjoy hand quilting as well."

JANE HARDY MILLER

This quilt contains an extensive collection of fabrics that are stitched in a number of 60-degree shape variations. The 60/20 degree diamond is the basis for the traditional quilt pattern Tumbling Blocks. By organizing the values of the fabrics into dark, medium, and light, and by keeping them consistently in the same position within the block, a strong, three-dimensional illusion was created. Jane has successfully given a contemporary slant to a complex quilt pattern. She worked from a vertical design wall, arranging and "auditioning" fabrics to ensure exactly the right positioning, and sometimes made sketches to plan the shape variations. Much of the machine quilting was done "freehand," with the feed dogs dropped. This quilt is exceptional for its judicious value placement, wide-ranging fabric combinations, and restrained palette.

Overall design

The main impression of this quilt, which is composed of interlocking diamonds and triangles in a number of different sizes and groupings, is its three-dimensional effect. The variety of both the shapes themselves and their different sizes encourages extended viewing.

Inspiration

This nineteenth-century Tumbling Blocks quilt made from silk clearly shows how, when three diamonds are stitched into a hexagon and the values are placed consistently, the illusion of a cube is created. The title of Jane's quilt, *Sixty Degrees and Falling*, acknowledges the traditional Tumbling Blocks pattern and alludes to the measurement of the angle in the diamond.

Small triangles

The areas of small triangles seem to merge into the larger shapes, shifting the levels of perception between two and three dimensions.

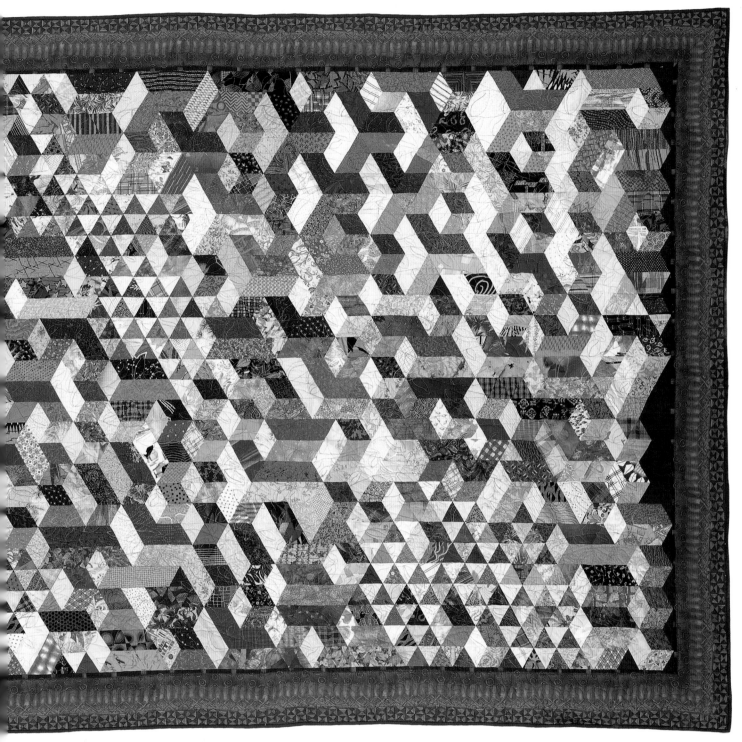

Graded fabrics

Fabrics have been skillfully graded by value to achieve the desired effect. A design wall enabled Jane to stand away from the work as it progressed to assess the effect.

Quilting

The quilting includes vines and other naturalistic designs, and was mainly stitched using free-motion quilting.

"BRUCH" FOLDED NINE

"I trained as an interior designer and in 1980 I began to study patchwork and quilting. I began by working with traditional patterns but soon began to develop my own designs. I love to work with paper, and to me it seems essential to play with a design in order to explore its full potential. I have been working with a simple block, such as a folded piece of paper, and a series of ten quilts is the result. I use mostly commercially available fabrics in plain colors. I teach patchwork and quilting and my work has been in exhibitions both at home in Germany and abroad and is also featured in various publications."

FRIEDERIKE KOHLHAUßEN

Friederike's series of "folded" quilts become increasingly complex as they progress. She began by folding squares of paper in numerous ways to create many designs. After making some of the quilts using traditional piecing methods, she introduced more experimental techniques for *"Bruch" Folded Nine*, including weaving strips of fabric, printing on the quilt surface, and using appliqué shapes to extend the design potential. A more complex design is superimposed on the underlying structure of a woven grid. The superimposed dark blue shapes contrast boldly, creating a dramatic impact. Working in series like this allows quilters to experiment with a number of design ideas, generating inspiration for future projects.

Overall design

The asymmetrical, woven checkerboard background is divided by bold, dark blue, horizontal chevrons and vertical squares. The brown strips, which seem to curve across the surface, create a three-dimensional illusion and serve to connect the background and foreground shapes.

Printing onto the quilt surface

The dots were printed onto the quilt surface before it was layered with the batting and after the strips had been woven to form the background.

Appliqué

The dark blue squares and chevrons were machine appliquéd onto the quilt, adding rhythmic complexities to the composition.

Fabric weaving

For the background, strips of torn fabric in different widths were woven together to create the checkerboard effect. Squares of fabric were appliquéd into some of the spaces between the woven strips.

Development of the design

To develop design ideas, Friederike makes multiple images on paper, which are then placed together in a number of different ways—sometimes even cut apart to create a design. In her "Folded" series, one part of the block looked like a folded square or a rooftop, and this gave the illusion of three dimensions in the quilt. When the design decisions have been made, the quilt is constructed using an appropriate combination of techniques.

WHIRLIGIG

"I started quiltmaking about 22 years ago, as I wanted to express myself in a medium that did not require a lot of expensive equipment. I was very interested in geometric shapes and color, and all that seemed to work really well in fabric. I have taken numerous classes with quiltmakers I admire, to learn different approaches and for inspiration. I need the challenge of working toward a deadline, such as an exhibition or competition, and find following a theme always makes me design something I never would have done before."

JANE LLOYD

Jane approached the design of this quilt by allowing the fabrics and techniques to spark shapes and ideas in her mind. First, the fabrics were sorted into value categories: dark, medium, light, and bright fabrics were grouped and strip-pieced with gently curved seams. When enough of this "created" fabric was ready, Jane cut wedge shapes, continuing the concept of curves, which led to the appearance of an irregular circle as she worked. Several of these circles were made. The end result was a quilt that communicates spontaneous freedom. There is an element of repetition, but the interweaving of wedges between the five "circles" presents the viewer with a chaotic order. The color scheme contributes to the exuberant effect.

Overall design

Five large, irregular circles spin and mingle, giving the impression of energetic movement. The highly contrasting color and value areas, in random strip widths, contribute to the effect. The patchwork dictates the irregular shape of the quilt—an inventive feature.

Binding

The irregular perimeter exhibits the same sense of freedom as the rest of the quilt.

Fabrics

The four main sets of fabrics, which were grouped in the first stage of construction, are interlaced across the surface of the quilt, connecting the circles.

Strips

Random strip widths were pieced together to create a fabric from which the wedge shapes were cut. The shapes were given curved or irregular wavy edges, which were matched to fit as construction progressed.

The blocks

Wedge-shaped pieces were randomly cut and pieced together in the manner of a Crazy Log Cabin. The resulting blocks were all different sizes and shapes, and so Jane devised a strategy for fitting them together by filling the gaps with more wedges. She comments, "I had a problem getting the whole quilt to lie flat; at one step I had to make a major tuck and do a lot of steam pressing."

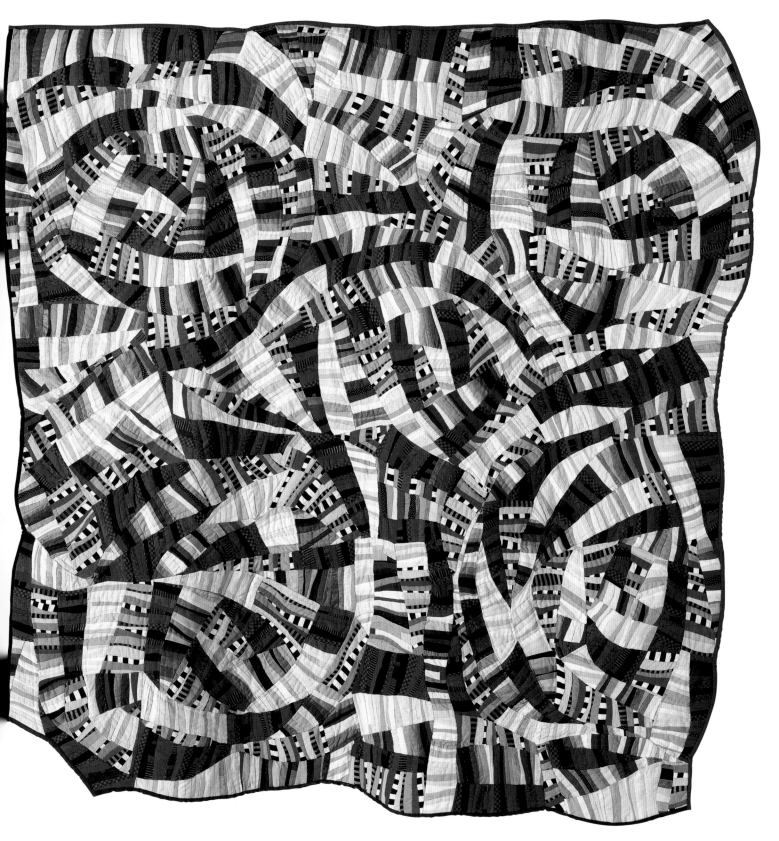

Size: 49 x 49 inches (124 x 124 cm)

BRISTOL STARS

"I visited Bristol Cathedral on a teaching trip to the U.K., and the cathedral's marble floor inspired this design. Mariner's Compass designs are my specialty and the floor has large, round spaces, some filled with stars. With the help of my husband and a computer, we adapted this by adding two concentric rings of Flying Geese, the outer one curved round the corner stars. The background grid was converted to squares drawn on a polar grid. In place of the stars on the floor, I used my favorite star designs. I worked out the color theory in advance, but it developed as I worked."

JUDY MATHIESON

The traditional Mariner's Compass pattern is extremely challenging to piece, and should only be undertaken by experienced quilters. Judy's love affair with the pattern has led her to write two books on the subject. In *Bristol Stars*, Judy set herself the challenge of perfecting the Mariner's Compass and extending this traditional design into a contemporary masterpiece of dazzling complexity. Its curved seams, narrow points, and intricate piecing show off Judy's expertise in complex construction, but her skill in arranging colors to blend harmoniously and give an illusion of transparency, especially in the large center star, is also evident. Subtle color differences in the grid of squares remind us of the variations found in polished marble.

Overall design

A large and complex central Mariner's Compass star is surrounded by two concentric rings of triangles. Between these, smaller stars are set over a grid of squares, which have been distorted to a polar grid. The problem of placing circular motifs into a square format is solved by looping the outer circle of triangles around the four corner compass stars, while the square grid continues to the outer edges.

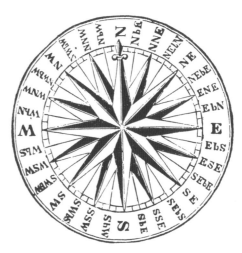

Mariner's compass

The wind roses on old sea charts may have inspired the early Mariner's Compass quilts, but a circle with radiating points is a common motif in many cultures. In nineteenth-century America, the quilt pattern was popular along the Eastern seaboard.

Size: 82 x 82 inches (208 x 208 cm)

Design and color work together in this dramatic quilt, providing variety and interest in every part of it. Symmetrical balance is offset by the inspired color choices. Details showcase the three radiating center stars, the corners, and some of the fabric choices for the medium-sized stars in the circle.

The large center motif is a series of concentric stars which increase in complexity from the center outward. The color gradations make the stars appear to spin.

Colors and shapes were integrated in the center stars, making the main compass points appear to be layers of transparent color, which subtly graduate through red, blue, and green.

Detail 2: Corner compasses

Looping the outer circle around the corner stars includes them in the main composition. The Flying Geese triangles flow smoothly from the larger circle around the smaller circles.

Detail 3: Fabrics

The fabrics were skillfully graded to flow from one color and value to another in every part of the quilt.

Accurate measurement and precision piecing were necessary to achieve the perfect symmetry required to fit all the elements of this quilt together.

Circular borders of Flying Geese motifs define the center compass and unify those set around it, including those at each corner.

Background grid

Although based on a grid of squares, each shape of the checkerboard had to have its own template, some of these were made using freezer paper for the templates. Every piece is different, and slight variations among the colors add further interest.

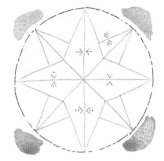

1 • Draft out the sections of the quilt to be pieced full size on freezer paper. Make color and value notes and registration marks in pencil to make piecing easier. Make a tracing.

2 • Cut the freezer paper along the lines and iron onto the right side of the fabrics. Cut the fabric around the template, adding ¼ inch (0.75cm) seam allowance.

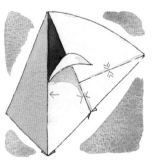

3 • Place fabrics right sides together, aligning the edges to be stitched. Stitch along the edges of the freezer paper, press seams, then peel away the templates.

KALEIDOSCOPIC XVI: MORE IS MORE

"My quilts combine the symmetry and surprise of a kaleidoscope with the techniques and materials of quiltmaking. There are two kinds of surprises: the meticulously planned kind and the happy coincidence. Making kaleidoscope quilts allows me to synthesize elements of both, merging control and spontaneity to spark something unexpected. I try to free myself from a conventional sense of fabric orderliness, seeking a random quality in order to imitate the succession of chance interlinkings and endless possibilities synonymous with kaleidoscopes."

PAULA NADELSTERN

Overall design

Four 12-sided, off-center mandalas are surrounded by 29 smaller ones that float in a field of rich colors dominated by a palette of burnt umber. Each displays a stunning kaleidoscopic pattern—magical temporary phenomena captured as textile heirlooms.

Fabric selection

Many of the fabrics Paula selected are printed cotton with an art nouveau influence in the design. Motifs have a bilateral symmetry in ordered repeats. Focus areas were created with the sheen of brightly colored silks.

The idea of taking the intricate images created by kaleidoscopes and transposing them into quilts demanded great skill and originality. Paula has studied state-of-the-art kaleidoscopes and claims that she is completely enticed by their magic. Here we see the light and color, form and motion of kaleidoscopic designs made in fabric. Intricate detail and inherent symmetry are achieved by working in units based on a "pie slice" section and repeating the same part of the printed fabric design in each wedge. The complexity of this quilt is the result of the fabrics within it. Pinpoints of light are simulated by sprinkling scraps of silk over the darker colors. Paula has created an explosion of visual excitement.

Kaleidoscopic patterns

The four larger mandalas in the center were made yet more complex by the addition of a patterned "shadow" that throws the symmetry off-center. This is the sixteenth quilt in a series that explores the endless possibilities synonymous with the patterns created in kaleidoscopes.

Working methods

Paula designs directly with her fabrics. Stitching lines and templates follow fabric choices, not the other way around. One full-size triangle drafted onto graph paper functioned as the blueprint for each kaleidoscope.

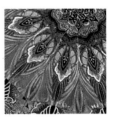

Effects

Although many of the designs are planned, Paula says, "Often effects more wonderful than I imagined occur." The use of harmonious fabrics for the setting of the circular images shows the circles off to maximum advantage.

Size: 64 x 64 inches (163 x 163 cm)

GLASS CARAFES

"I was a painter before I came to quiltmaking. I studied quiltmaking with Michael James and he encouraged me back into designing my own art. I started by making traditional quilts, then worked through a number of style changes. I used the mandala, circular symbols of the universe from Oriental art and religion, as a design inspiration. This was followed by dimensional quilts and subsequently those which investigate isometric perspectives. In both of these, illusions of three dimension are created by the use of graduated tones—dark through to light. At present I am enjoying landscapes and still life, and feel I have returned full circle to my beginnings as a painter."

KATIE PASQUINI MASOPUST

Since becoming a quiltmaker, Katie has established a reputation for exploring and inventing new techniques to demonstrate her unique style. In *Glass Carafes*—a still life on fabric—her origins as a painter are evident. Two circles are superimposed on the quilt, and the shapes within these fractured circles pick up the reflections that bounce off the glass, adding to the illusion and sparkle. The strength of the composition is in the dramatic shift from the illuminated objects in the foreground to the darker colors in the background. Skillful handling of perspective gives the image solidity in which light, color, and space fuse.

Overall design

Four glass carafes are depicted standing on a table surrounded by draped fabrics. Details of the objects, such as the angular facets of the glass stoppers, are realistically depicted. But the realism is combined with an overlay of more abstract shapes to graphic effect. Expert machine appliqué and machine quilting produced this incredible piece of fiber art.

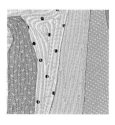

Fabrics

The fabrics used have a variety of visual textures and patterns. Narrow stripes, dots, and solids have been used effectively.

Inspiration

Katie set up this still life, just as a painter would, to use as her template. Her exact reproduction of it in quilt form is impressive.

Pictorial details

Small pieces of fabric were used in a free-form collage approach to build up realistic images of the glass.

Circular overlays

Light and shade are skillfully used to create the circular overlay, containing shapes that echo the reflective texture of the glass.

Size: 39 x 57 inches (99 x 145 cm)

SEVEN QUILTS

"I began with the idea of several quilts thrown across a bed. I wanted to use fabrics with both large- and small-scale prints and to include a mixture of geometric, floral, abstract, traditional, and contemporary patterns. I put them together in such a way that the appearance is of several different quilts, and yet they all combine in a whole new harmonious surface. The quilt was made for an exhibition with the overall title Layers of Inspiration. *The design of the quilt speaks for itself."*

SHEILA YALE

The interpretation of a specific theme for exhibitions will always stretch the creative imagination. Here, Sheila has risen admirably to the challenge with an exotic mixture of patterned fabrics that produce a rich visual texture. There are a number of traditional piecing designs, all juxtaposed to create a quilt with a lively composition full of spirited originality. As a trained textile designer, Sheila is very aware of the potential inherent in commercially available fabrics for her vibrant quilts. She began making patchwork while she was a student because it allowed her to use up scraps of beautiful printed fabrics, preserving them and giving them a permanent showcase. This is still her stated motivation for quiltmaking and in this piece she has succeeded admirably.

Overall design
This is a cleverly integrated composition of patterns that suggests an illusion in the manner of a trompe l'oeil painting. Black and white or high-contrast prints have been used to separate the different areas of the quilt and underline the individuality of the different "quilts" within it.

Pieced patterns
Flying Geese, Nine Patch, Strips, and Triangles are among the traditional pieced patterns that make up the quilt.

Illusion

In order to continue the illusion of layered quilts, the edges of the second "quilt" have been allowed to overlap the border of the first.

Quilting

The quilt has been hand quilted using colored threads that complement the patches and the patterned fabrics.

Borders

Each "quilt" features different-sized patches and printed patterns and is separated from its neighbors by a high-contrast border.

Fabric selection

One of Sheila's stylistic hallmarks is her ability to identify unusual fabrics and successfully combine them, mixing scale and style in her own recognizable formula.

Size: 95 x 105 inches (241 x 267 cm)

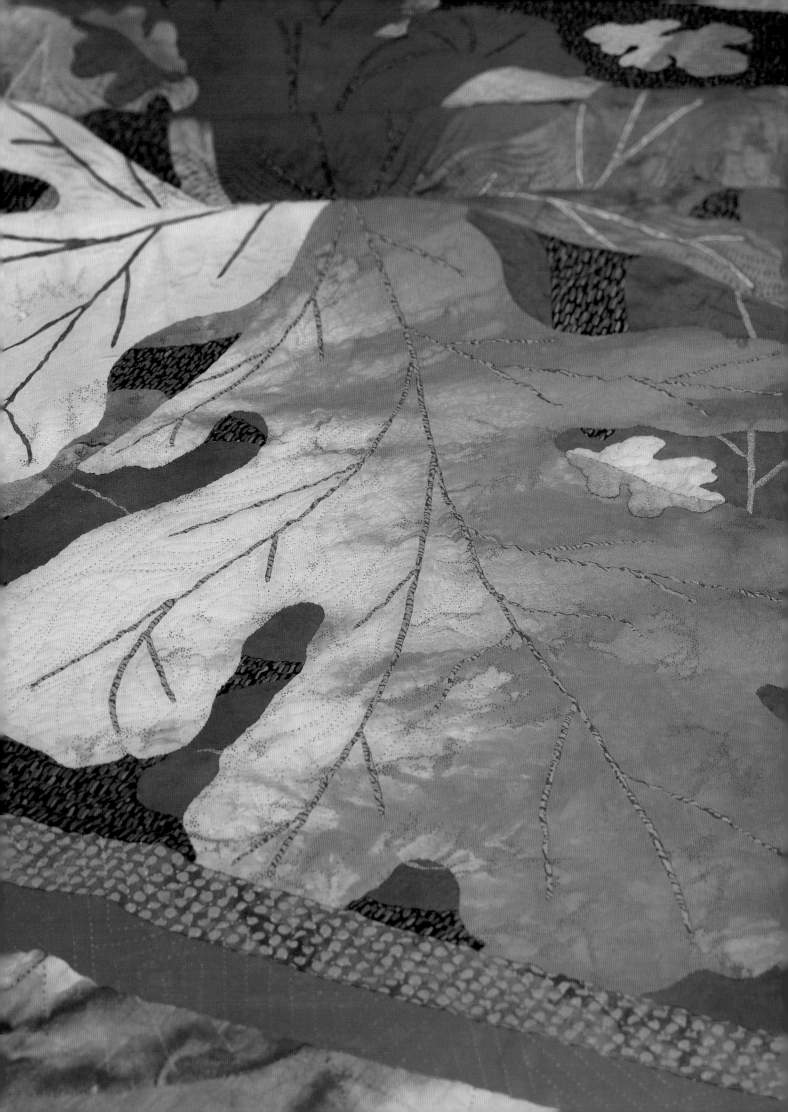

PICTORIAL AND STORY

No longer simply regarded as the means to produce a functional object, quiltmaking has been embraced as a medium that allows artists to express an idea or belief. Choosing fabric and thread as their tools, and often combining traditional and innovative techniques, fiber artists aim to communicate. The quilts in this chapter are not just beautiful and intricate works of art; each also has a riveting story to tell or an important message to convey.

TEA FOR TROUT = TROUT FOR TEA

"This quilt is one in a series of over 70 quilts called Menagerie. *The series' focus is endangered animals and the need for responsible actions on the part of humans to preserve and nurture the habitat. My quilts are a soapbox from which I express my opinions. I view making a quilt as a journey. Each step is one toward the destination. The destination is the journey, or, in other words, you gain true knowledge of art through making it."*

MARTA AMUNDSON

Overall design

Randomly repeated fish silhouettes float in the center section of the quilt. The background is full of surface interest and texture created by printing, dyeing, and quilting. A crisp, irregular, black and white, sawtooth border separates the inner section from the broad outer border, but this is breached in places by the floating fish shapes, linking the center panel with the border. The combination of techniques displays an admirable control of the medium of contemporary fiber design.

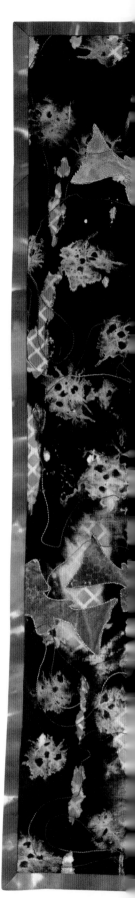

A number of color techniques were combined in the making of this quilt. The dye from black cotton was discharged with bleach by printing with the end of a spool, then combined with hand-dyed and airbrushed cotton canvas. The fish shapes were fused onto the background. A fine nylon net was added as a fourth layer to protect the raw edges of the canvas and to prevent fraying. The design developed when Marta realized that the negative space that was left when the trout shapes were cut from the canvas was as interesting as the fish themselves. By repeating elements of the design across the work, and exploiting those negative spaces, both figurative and abstract imagery is used to convey the message that there will be no fish left if we take their water and habitat.

Color study

Marta has restricted her color palette to dark shades enlivened by brighter oranges and greens, but these are still in the medium/dark value range. The only pale fabric is used in the inner border.

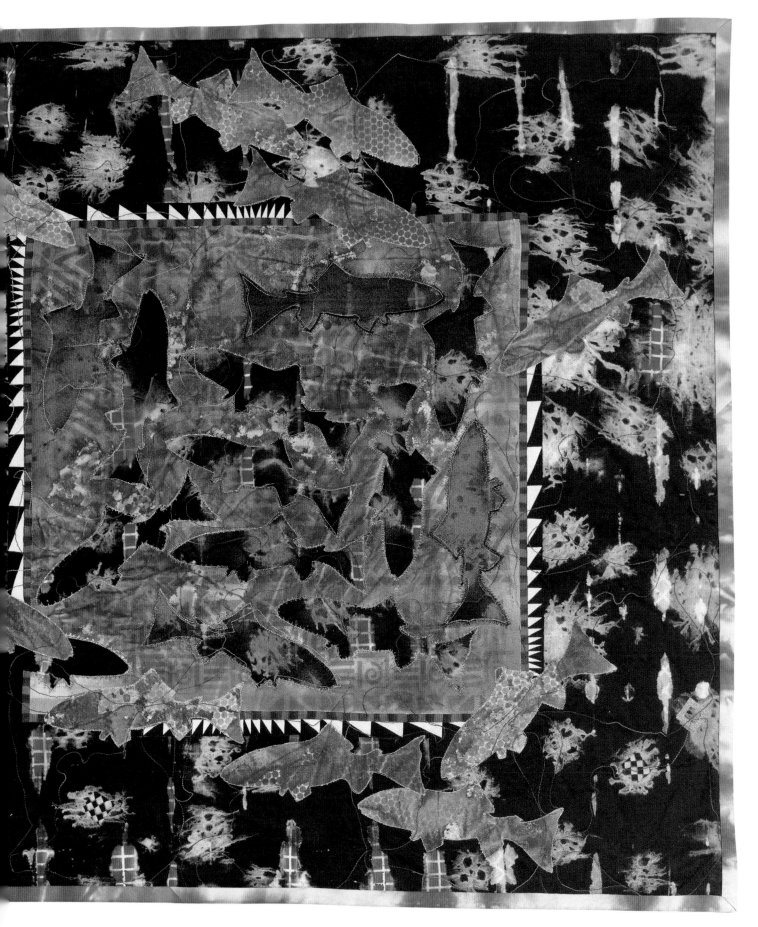

Size: 34 x 32 inches (86 x 81 cm)

Tea for Trout = Trout for Tea 67

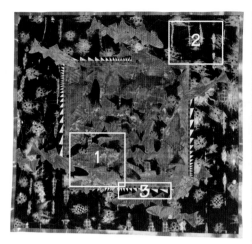

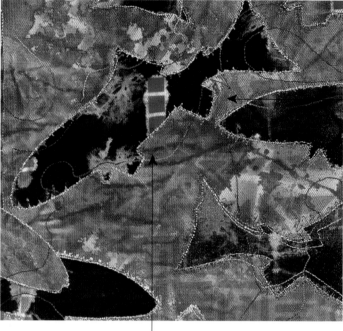

The repetitive trout and teapot shapes were quilted, and metallic decorative stitches outline the fish.

Bobbin stitching, a protective layer of net, and a contrasting sawtooth border are among the numerous techniques used in the construction of this quilt.

When using a thick thread for machine quilting, the thread must be wound onto the bobbin and the pattern stitched from the back. To guide the stitching design, a freezer paper template was ironed onto the back of the quilt, then the quilting was stitched on the backing, so the bobbin thread effectively became the top thread.

Detail 2: Net layer & color

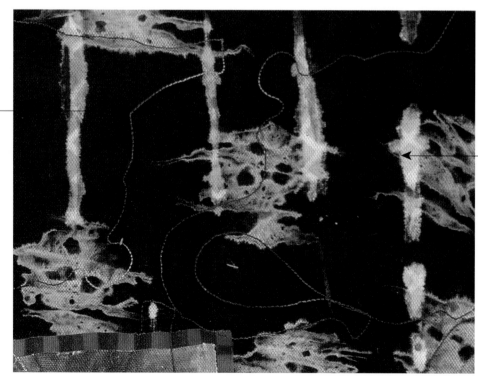

The top layer of the quilt—a fine nylon net—holds the separate elements together. It is hardly noticeable, but it fulfills the necessary function of preserving the quilt.

Marta added additional color to the background by spraying acrylic airbrush paint through hardware cloth.

Detail 3: Sawtooth border

A narrow red and black strip complements the crisp black and white triangles.

The inner section of the quilt is separated from the outer border by strips of irregular black and white sawtooth triangles. These provide an effective foil to the organic fish shapes.

TECHNIQUES FOR PRINTING SURFACE DESIGN ON FABRIC

"Found" objects such as corks, wooden buttons, leaves, thread spools, and cards can be used to print onto fabric. Simple printing blocks can be carved from half a potato or an eraser to make a series of marks.

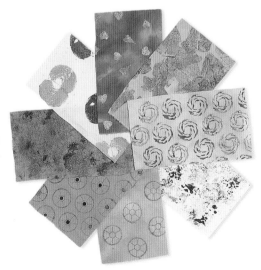

1 • To prepare the fabric dyes for printing, thicken them with sodium alginate. To discharge the color from the fabric, use thickened bleach instead of fabric dye. Mix the dye paint or bleach in a shallow container, dab a scrunched-up rag or sponge in the paint and press onto the surface of the fabric, using even, allover pressure.

2 • When selecting an object to print from, the printing surface should be smooth and on one plane. Brush the dye onto the printing surface, either with a paintbrush or roller, or make an inkpad by saturating an absorbent surface, such as several layers of felted blanket, with the dye. Apply an even coating of ink to the printing block, then press the print block firmly and steadily on the fabric surface. Experiment with designs on paper before using the blocks on the fabric.

3 • Try spraying dye paint through stencils, or over torn cardboard, leaves, chicken wire, or coiled string to make interesting patterns. Spatter patterns can be created by dipping an old toothbrush in dye and flicking the bristles a short distance from the fabric.

Mom's Bread

"For 18 years I have made a special homemade bread. It's our staple, a high protein, wholewheat bread that my children have been raised on. My husband especially loves it, and worried that if something were to happen to me, he wouldn't know how to make it. So, I photographed the bread in progress, made it into a quilt and placed the recipe on the back! Now he has a permanent record of the bread in his quilt."

SANDY BONSIB

The sequence of photographs detailing the stages of breadmaking were transferred onto fabric using an innovative technique—photo-transfer. Then, each photograph was made into a simple block with the addition of strips stamped with lettering, made with a rubber stamp alphabet and fabric paint. Folksy plaids and stripes were used for the surrounding blocks, which were made simply from squares and triangles. A secondary design of diamonds forms a background to the picture blocks and adds complexity. After writing her book *Quilting Your Memories*, in which many contributors submitted work that commemorated major events in their lives, Sandy decided to make this quilt as a tribute to an everyday happening, a celebration of the mundane which often goes unrecorded. The quilt as a symbol of home and family is extended here.

Overall design

A sequence of nine blocks explains, using photo-transfers and simply printed instructions, how to make Sandy's homemade bread. Blocks made from squares and triangles frame the photos. The design was machine quilted by Becky Kraus.

Fabric selection

The choice of plaids and stripes adds to the connotations of homespun simplicity, stressing the nostalgic value of connecting with past quilters.

Recipe

The bread recipe on the back of the quilt emphasizes the quilt's dual function: to provide both warmth and wholesome nourishment.

Photo-transfer of images onto fabric

Photographs can be copied onto fabric using a special transfer paper. First make a color copy of the image and a mirror image of the original so that it transfers the right way round on the fabric. Place the transfer paper in the copier's paper drawer and copy the image onto it. Position the transfer paper on a piece of tightly woven fabric with right sides facing and iron the image onto the fabric.

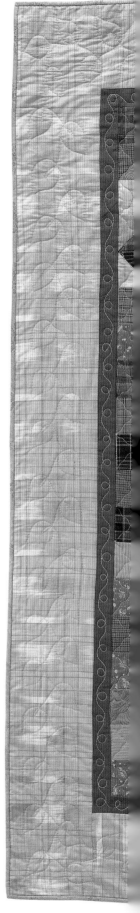

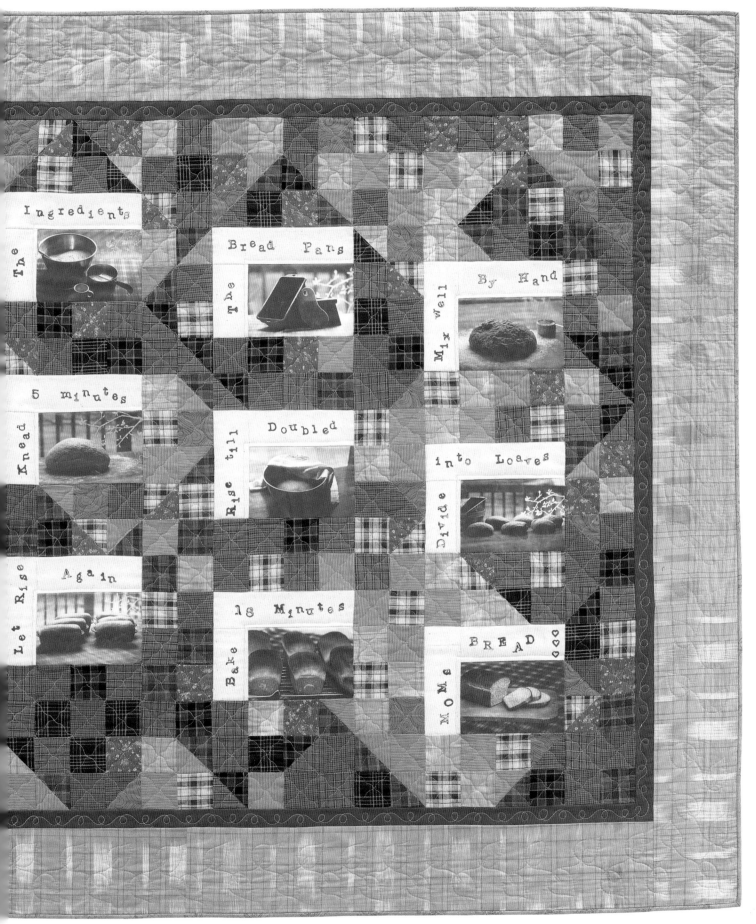

BITTERSWEET II

"*Bittersweet II is one of a series of quilts using fall tree imagery. My recent return to tree imagery follows much abstract work using torn fabric, directly appliquéd. There is a return to tighter construction methods, such as the use of seams which protect the cut edge of the fabric. This tree imagery differs from my earlier work in its ethereal quality, created by using paint and organza fabric. I feel these trees echo my interest in both the inner and outer selves and the ensuing dialogue between the two.*"

ERIKA CARTER

Overall design
A composition of painted trees is superimposed onto a background of broad, vertical columns. Subtle color changes are created by hand painting, but the seams joining the columns are hard-edged, to contrast with the free drawing of the trees—silhouetted, they contrast starkly with the incandescent background.

Floating leaves
The floating orange shapes give an impression of leaves by association—they are more abstract than realistic in character.

Natural imagery is a major influence in Erika's quilts, especially that of trees and the healing qualities of nature. She has worked through various styles of quiltmaking. Here, she has abandoned earlier techniques of strip-pieced backgrounds in favor of a freer approach—that of hand painting a background of combined cotton and silk organza, onto which floating shapes are directly hand appliquéd. The glowing colors of the background, pieced in broad vertical sections, form a canvas for the hand painted trees. The addition of the semi-abstract leaf shapes, which float over the whole surface, add movement. The impression is one of regret for the last golden rays of sunshine that occur on fall days.

Inspiration
The rich shades of fall foliage in a New England woodland are reflected in *Bittersweet II*.

SIZE: 69 X 51 INCHES (175 X 129 CM)

Trees

Artistic confidence is evident in the freehand painting of the trees onto the background. Erika uses the image of the trees as a metaphor for strength.

Background seaming

The seams that join the background fabric are an integral part of the composition, underlining the vertical emphasis established by the trees.

BIRD STUDY #4

"Each of these birds could have woven together their nests faster than I did; it just gives you an added appreciation of nature's ways. I am led by a piece of fabric wherever it takes me—pulled into action by the feel and mood of the fiber. I am not interested in recreating a photographic scene: I want to juxtapose realism, only insofar as it intrigues me, using symbolic fabrics to produce summarized forms and suggested textures. I want my simple forms to breathe a bit, and so cause you, too, to breathe a bit and say 'Oh, yes, it IS beautiful out there.'"

JOAN COLVIN

Joan Colvin began her art career in painting and drawing. When she discovered quiltmaking in 1988, she was able to combine her lifelong love of fabric with her fine art skills. In her bird studies she has taken a mixed media approach, combining collage-like machine appliqué, using hard and soft edges, with machine quilting. She also changes the surface at will, by using fabric pens, fabric paints, threads, beads, and other embellishments. She will use any technique, any approach that evokes the flavor of her vision. Her aim is for "fluidity—relaxed realism to represent the meandering lines of nature, the shapes that have worn and evolved over time." Joan is internationally known for her use of subdued colors and for her designs inspired by nature.

Overall design

A bird is depicted perching on its nest, which clings precariously to a realistic cracked and fissured rock face. The nest, complete with eggs, is created using a collage technique and various fabrics, including ribbon, raffia, and silk strips.

The bird

As the bird is camouflaged against the darker section of the rock, the viewer must work quite hard to make out the bird's outline. Joan says of the birds, "You may or may not recognize the birds .... I might be inclined to try for authenticity ... but sometimes an unknown slips in and I can't let him get away."

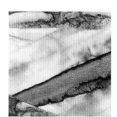

The rock face

To represent the rock face a range of monochromatic fabrics in shades of gray through black were folded and pressed to give the impression of a fissured surface. The illusion was further enhanced with textile paints.

The nest

The nest provides a change in color from the monochromatic rock. Mixed media techniques were used to convey the textures of the twigs and straw.

FABRIC COLLAGE: MAKING THE NEST

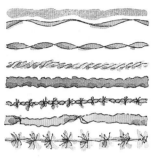

1 • Make a collection of assorted fibers; these could include raffia, ribbons, cut and frayed strips of fabric, and string.

2 • On the surface of the quilt top, arrange the fibers horizontally and secure to the surface with small stitches from the back. Machine appliqué egg shapes directly over the nest fibers.

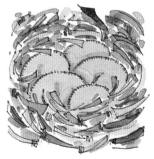

3 • Stiffen the nest fibers with spray starch, then twist and weave them together. Fix the fibers in place with stitches and knots. Poke small twigs and bits of straw beween the fibers. Finish with more spray starch to hold the collage in shape.

SIZE: 40 X 50 INCHES (102 X 127 CM)

REGENERATION, MOUNT ST. HELENS

"Having been interested in Mount St. Helens since its eruption on May 18th, 1980, I seized the opportunity to visit the place in 1992. Driving up onto the mountain through established forests, which were interrupted by areas bearing increasing signs of the devastation caused, was impressive. Standing on the mountain was more awe inspiring than beautiful. I wanted to make a quilt about it because I felt that it could convey the feeling of both the disaster and the subsequent regeneration of the landscape over a period of time. How to set about doing it was a question that kept me puzzling for three years."

JENNI DOBSON

Jenni's aim was to make an expressive quilt that would awaken reactions in the viewer similar to her own at the destruction of a beautiful landscape and the power of nature to regenerate and recover. Jenni used a number of techniques to express her ideas. She worked directly with the fabrics, with no preliminary sketches or designs; she found this to be risky but ultimately rewarding, and the work of piecing the top went surprisingly quickly. The difficulty of combining traditional and innovative techniques was considerable and took a degree of conviction. Her personal vision was to convey and express the story of Mount St. Helens, here admirably realized.

Overall design

Jenni pieced the background in the form of one large, modified Delectable Mountains block, which provides an underlying traditional structure. The exploded mountain top is suggested by inserting triangular, strip-pieced intercut sections. Fragmented Log Cabin blocks and skewed Maple Leaf blocks represent the effects of the disaster on the homes and forests of the local community.

Inspiration

Jenni's quilt tells the story of the devastation caused by the eruption of Mount St. Helens and the area's subsequent regeneration.

Skewed blocks

Maple Leaf blocks are pieced into their squares at a slanting angle to give them a windswept appearance.

Quilting

A quilting pattern with curved lines was used in the landscape area, suggesting a calmer environment where the regeneration is taking place.

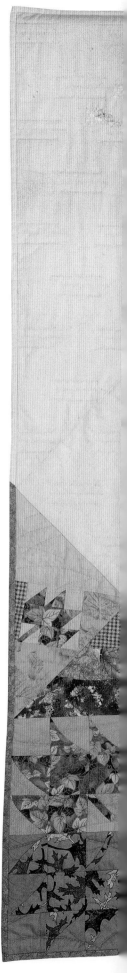

SIZE: 48 X 48 INCHES (122 X 122 CM)

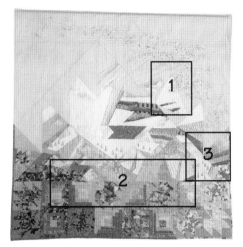

Detail 1: Fragmentation

The ash cloud is represented by confetti appliqué—tiny snips of fabric scattered onto the surface and held down with free-motion machine stitches.

A variety of techniques has been used to communicate the story of Mount St. Helens, and they have been successfully combined to present the full picture. Details show in close-up how Jenni used traditional and innovative techniques to achieve the result she was aiming for.

The modified Delectable Mountains block was intercut with strip-pieced sections, some of which have raw-edge inserts to suggest fragmentation. Quilting in short, straight lines gives the impression of a disturbed atmosphere.

Trees cut with pinking shears and applied to the quilt like Band-Aids symbolically suggest the power of nature to recover and regenerate.

Detail 2: Eruption & regeneration

Reverse seaming—sewing the wrong sides of the pieces together—was used in some of the small Log Cabin blocks, introducing ragged edges to indicate the homes destroyed by the eruption.

A border on the lower edge uses a combination of Log Cabin and windswept Maple Leaf blocks and shows the ash-covered scene on the right-hand side and the regeneration of woods and farms on the left.

Detail 3: Fabric selection

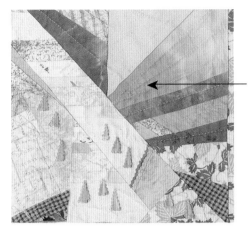

Jenni started her project by collecting fabrics that had prints reminiscent of landscape and geology. Spray-dyeing extended the collection even more. A subdued color palette of grays, neutrals, and greens was deliberately selected to evoke the natural world the quilt aims to represent.

REVERSE-SEAM LOG CABIN BLOCKS

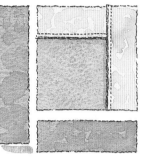

1 • Sort printed fabrics into dark and light values. Tear strips 1 inch (2.5 cm) wide along the crosswise grain. Cut a 2 inch (5 cm) dark square for the center. With wrong sides together, stitch two light strips to adjacent sides of the square as shown. Using a brush, fray the raw edges of the seams. Stitch two dark strips to the remaining sides of the square, fraying the raw edges.

2 • Continue adding strips, fraying the edges, and keeping the dark and light strips diagonally opposite, until there are three or four rounds. Brush the completed block with a dry brush to further fray the edges.

Label

On the back of the quilt a label, also in the form of a Delectable Mountains block, is stitched into the quilt, telling the story of how it came to be made.

STRIP-PIECED PANEL WITH TORN-STRIP INSERTS

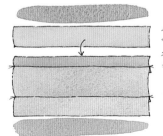 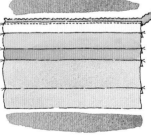 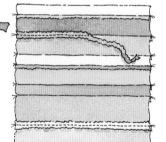 

1 • Cut strips of fabric about 12 inches (30 cm) long and of varying widths between ½ to 1½ inches (1½ to 4 cm), and stitch them together along the long edges to make squares.

2 • Join the squares to make panels, inserting torn strips of fabric between the joining seams so that a raw edge of each strip will be exposed.

3 • After completing a panel, lay additional torn strips over it as desired. Stitch along the center of each strip to secure.

4 • Cut segments from the strip-pieced panel to use in pieced blocks.

PATCHWORK WATERLILIES

"I took my first quilting class 22 years ago to sharpen my sewing skills. Quite frankly, I thought quilts were old and raggedy and I couldn't imagine why anyone would want to spend their time making one. I guess I have changed my mind; I quilt now because it allows me to express myself in a medium that I have always loved—fiber. There are so many facets to quilting that the variety and the ideas are virtually limitless. No matter how many quilts I make there are always more ideas in my mind for the next one."

ANN FAHL

During the course of her quilt-making career Ann Fahl has created a distinguished body of work. Her hallmark is to combine a pieced background and appliqué with decorative machine stitching and beading. Ann constructed the background of the quilt using a technique that she terms "free form" patchwork. After the inner and outer borders were added, the completed background was steam pressed and squared up. The water lilies and pads were appliquéd, then the quilt was machine embroidered. The addition of dragonflies provided the finishing touch. A small sprinkling of clear, iridescent seed beads was added around the top of each water lily to provide interest. The machine quilting is simple, so as not to detract from the piecing.

Overall design

A composition of water lilies was appliquéd onto a pieced background. The pictorial elements were positioned in the center of the quilt: the size of the lilies and pads was graduated to create perspective. The striped inner border contains the pond elements, with the dynamic exception of one lily pad.

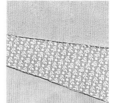

Construction of the background

Ann pieced the vertical, wedge-shape background sections on a foundation of non-woven interfacing. Foundation piecing allowed her to create textural surface interest and include pictorial details such as the spiky leaves.

A neat finish

One advantage of constructing the strip-pieced sections on a foundation was that the seams were contained inside the quilt top, between the pieced top and the foundation.

SIZE: 32½ x 27½ INCHES (83 x 70 CM)

SPIKY WATER LILY LEAVES

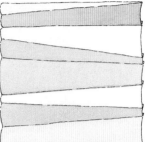

1 • Draw a water lily design onto foundation fabric, marking which pieces are background and which are leaves. Decide on a logical piecing order and number the shapes accordingly.

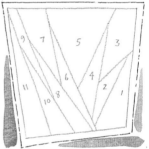

2 • Using strips that finish between ½ to 1½ inches (1.5 to 4 cm) wide, make a strip-pieced panel large enough to accommodate all the background segments, including generous seam allowances.

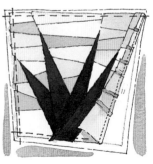

3 • Sew the shapes to the foundation (see page 43), cutting the background segments from the strip-pieced panel.

Embroidery

The dragonflies' wings have been heavily embroidered with gold thread, while their bodies are embellished with a dark, metallic thread twisted with black.

GINKGO BILOBA

"Natural subjects are the focus of most of my quilts and this was inspired by the ginkgo tree. Although nature was the starting point, it was as much an exploration of the piecing medium and my eclectic collection of fabrics as it is a depiction of the ginkgo. The part of quilting I enjoy most is designing and fabric selection."

RUTH B. MCDOWELL

R uth B. McDowell has had a distinguished career as a quiltmaker. She is known for her dazzling images and creative use of fabric, and in *Ginkgo Biloba* we are not disappointed. Her interpretation of the ginkgo, an ornamental tree native to China, makes effective use of fabrics to depict a close view of fan-shaped leaves. Eye-catching plaids and stripes are teamed with a collection of yellow floral and textured fabrics. These large leaf shapes are pieced into a dark background collage for maximum visual impact. Ruth uses innovative piecing techniques to achieve the desired results, and color choices were made from the fabrics in her extensive collection. The quilting is free-motion machine stitching "drawn" directly with the machine, without any previous marking.

Overall design
Large, fan-shaped leaves set against a background of rich colors fuses striking design with bold contrast. Directional fabrics add to the illusion of folds, creating a dialogue between flat surface and spatial depth.

Piecing technique
To prepare for piecing, Ruth drafted a full-size "cartoon" of her design, and then made a template for each piece.

Quilting
Free-motion quilting adds to the surface texture of the quilt, giving selected areas greater definition.

PIECING CURVED SEAMS

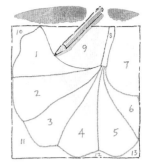

1 • Draw the design full size on Bristol paper. Make a tracing. Number the pieces of the design in the order they will be stitched together, both on the original drawing and on the tracing.

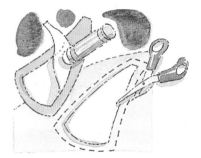

2 • Cut the drawing apart on the dividing lines. Place the shapes onto the fabrics; then cut ¼ inch (0.75 cm) around the shape for seam allowances. Or, make a template with added seam allowance by glueing the paper pieces to larger pieces of paper and cutting ¼ inch (0.75 cm) extra all around.

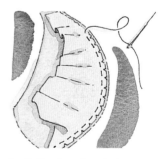

3 • Following the piecing sequence, stitch the fabrics together. Clip into the seam allowances along concave curves to help ease the curves to fit.

UMBRELLA THORN TREE

"I trained as a home economics teacher, and have taught dressmaking, tailoring, and machine embroidery. I experimented with quiltmaking in the mid-1970s but seriously started in the late 1980s. I now teach machine quilting and machine appliqué full-time. I have always loved sewing machines and have challenged myself to do on the sewing machine what others do by hand. This piece brings back wonderful memories of a trip to South Africa in 1996."

MAURINE NOBLE

Overall design

Here, the medium of quiltmaking is used to create a textile painting. The fabrics chosen for the disparate elements—a mixture of hand-dyed cotton, commercial prints, and South African textiles—are perfect, the textured batiks working well with the large-scale abstract prints to interpret the landscape. The free-motion machine quilting, stitched in fluid curves, unifies the separate areas of the composition and adds surface texture.

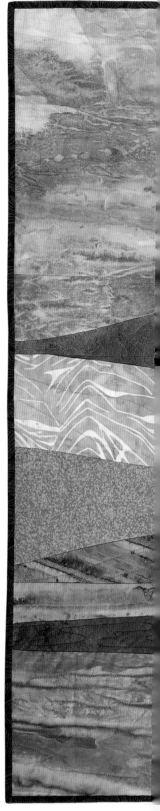

Using a collection of cotton fabrics Maurine has created an evocative landscape. There is an element of formal simplification in the composition that increases the impact of this dramatic scene. The main foreground image of the tree is set against distant mountains. The broad border, rather than just acting as a frame, contrives to be a continuation of the picture, thanks to a clever value shift that creates a sort of transparency. As a result, the central image seems to glow, fusing color, light, and space. Maurine studied the piecing methods used in this quilt with Ruth B. McDowell (see page 82.) After drawing the design full size on paper, Maurine made templates for piecing. The perfectly executed narrow strips and sharp points command our admiration, but the quilt succeeds as much for its expressive qualities as for its technical virtuosity.

Inspiration

This landscape of South Africa and, in particular, memories retained in a picture taken in Shakaland, were the inspiration behind *Umbrella Thorn Tree.*

Fabric scale

The use of a large-scale print in the shadow area and in the lower foliage of the tree provides a shifting focus between the tree in the foreground and the landscape behind.

SIZE: 38½ X 32 INCHES (98 X 81 CM)

Quilting

Maurine says that she "loves to machine quilt." Here her expertise is displayed perfectly in the fluid overall stitching that covers the surface of the quilt.

Border frame

By offsetting a seam line, or by using a subtle shift in value between the center section and the border, the frame forms a retreating backdrop—a depiction of the far distance.

THE GREEK QUILT

"A thesis I wrote at college on 'The Representation of the Human Figure on Greek Pots' formed the initial inspiration for the design. The pots inspired the colors I used, and visual texture was created by using marble patterned fabrics. The female figures on the left were derived from women mourners on a funeral vase. Here they symbolize the trials and tribulations of making a quilt. On the right, however, the dancing figures represent the feeling of joy quilters have on the completion of a piece of work. Between the two groups a miniature quilt is held up for display. This is the longest I have spent on a quilt—533 hours."

SHEENA NORQUAY

This quilt uses a combination of techniques—machine piecing, hand appliqué, beading, and free-motion machine embroidery and quilting. The main panel is placed slightly above the middle of the quilt to imitate the composition of scenes painted on amphorae. The panel placement establishes a balanced background onto which the motifs are appliquéd, providing the rhythmic repetition typical of the decorations on Greek pots. Human figures, birds, and animals are reduced to geometric shapes, which form bands of repetitive patterns. Variation in the border widths, motif sizes, and color placement add interest to the repetitive patterns. Sheena has created a veritable textile tour de force.

Overall design

The combination of pictorial and geometric motifs gives this quilt plenty of interest. Elements of the composition are bound together by a series of rectangles that form a background for the inventive interpretations of the Greek theme. The repetition of the picture in the main panel—two birds facing each other—on the miniature quilt below is an intriguing feature.

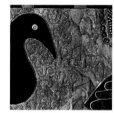

Appliqué

The motifs are stitched onto the background using traditional needle-turned appliqué, and embellished with beading and embroidered details.

Quilting

A number of free-motion machine quilting designs create rich texture on the surface of the quilt. The distinctions between embroidery and quilting are blurred by the use of machine embroidery stitches in combination with the quilting.

Inspiration

It was a study of the decoration of ancient Greek pots, in particular the depiction of birds and figures combined with decorative patterns, that inspired Sheena to create this quilt.

Background

The organization of the pieced background provides spaces that are ideal for the stylized figure, bird, and flower motifs. These spaces are skillfully linked by repeated abstract patterns.

Size: 66 x 83 inches (168 x 211 cm)

EVEN CHANGE

"When I found quiltmaking I realized it fulfilled all the needs I had creatively. Even Change is the fourth in a series of leaf designs inspired by the trees in and around the area where I live. My view is that we are not separate from nature but a part of it, and I want to bring the viewer back into the world in which we live—to dispel the feeling of alienation many of us have. For me, the process is the joy. I would rather make fewer quilts from which I learn many things, than many quilts from which I learn nothing."

GABRIELLE SWAIN

This design was developed as a color study of temperature. No attention was paid to hue or value, only the temperature of the color—warm or cool. Gabrielle began the quilt by working out the design on paper, finding the act of putting pencil to paper both comforting and exciting. Many of her quilts are designed over a long period of time, but she found that *Even Change* "worked itself." The leaves were applied using both regular and reverse appliqué, the latter being used to depict the narrow leaf veins. For the double inner borders, Gabrielle selected colors to harmonize with the leaf fabrics. Swirling lines of hand quilting complement the leaf shapes. This combination of techniques has produced an arresting quilt with an impression of a floating backdrop.

Overall design

The quilt surface is divided into four large sections, each of which has both large- and small-scale leaf shaped appliqués. A double, narrow inner border interchanges colors at the corners and divides the large center panel from the outer border, which includes leaves worked in the smaller scale. Bright colors combined with large shapes provide maximum impact.

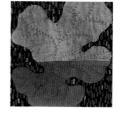

Inspiration

Many quilters look to the natural world and their immediate environment for inspiration. Gabrielle explains, "working with designs from the backyard and the area where I live helps bring me closer to my specific part of the world."

Counterchange

The four center sections of the quilt are defined not only by their background colors, but also by changing the colors of the motifs that are superimposed over the dividing lines. The changing colors of the inner borders continue this design device.

Quilting

A quilting thread in a contrasting color was used to add definition and texture to the large leaf shapes.

Size: 52 x 52 inches (132 x 132 cm)

NARROW REVERSE APPLIQUÉ

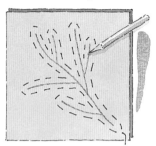

1 • Draw the pattern onto the right side of the top fabric, using single lines. Place the top fabric over the vine fabric. Baste ⅜ inch (1 cm) away from the lines.

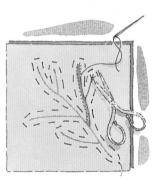

2 • Make a 2 to 3 inch (5 to 8 cm) cut along the line. Turn under the raw edge along one side and stitch it to the background fabric. Continue cutting and stitching in short segments, appliquéing one side of the stem completely before beginning the other side.

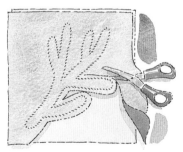

3 • When the stitching is finished, turn the work over and cut away the excess vine fabric.

VEILED

"I began quiltmaking with a sampler quilt class in 1986 and progressed through workshops, design classes, and masterclasses. My primary motivation was that I understood fabric as a medium. The aspect of quilting I most enjoy is design—to use it as a form of personal expression. I made this quilt to celebrate the strong pioneer women of my family: their stories half-remembered, perhaps never fully told. Ambitions, desires, hopes, jealousies would all have been veiled by the laws of ladylike behavior."

PAM WINSEN

Here, the expressive potential of the quilt bridges the gap between craft and fine art. Using a mixture of materials and techniques, *Veiled* provokes thoughts about the lives of previous generations of women. Pam photocopied her mother's wedding dress and used the copies to make a full-size collage. The collage was photo-transferred onto silk georgette—the same fabric as the original gown—that had first been dyed with tea to "age" it. The next stage was to mount the fabric on canvas and embellish it with beads, hand quilting, muslin, and paint. Aged mulberry paper was used for the border because of its similarity to old photographs. A wedding dress can symbolize youth and hope for the future, but here it brings the past alive as graphically as antique, sepia-tinted photographs.

Overall design

The flimsy fabric onto which the image of the dress was transferred became distorted into pleats and folds. The dress shape was decorated with fragments of embroidery, quilting, and beading. Loosely woven muslin threads overlaid in some areas suggest the deterioration caused by the passing of time. These overflow onto the frame giving a visual reference to the title *Veiled*.

Muslin

Muslin threads have been unraveled and applied to parts of the main composition and the frame to depict cobwebs, and to imply the passage of time and decay.

Quilting

Hand quilting using a heavy silk thread was used to emphasize the pleats and folds in the background.

Embroidery

The embroidered flower motifs provide a flash of color in an otherwise neutral palette. Further detail was added with beads and stenciled leaves.

Inspiration

Pam's mother's wedding dress— its symbolic importance, its place in history, and even its fabric—inspired a quilt that gives us a glimpse of the past.

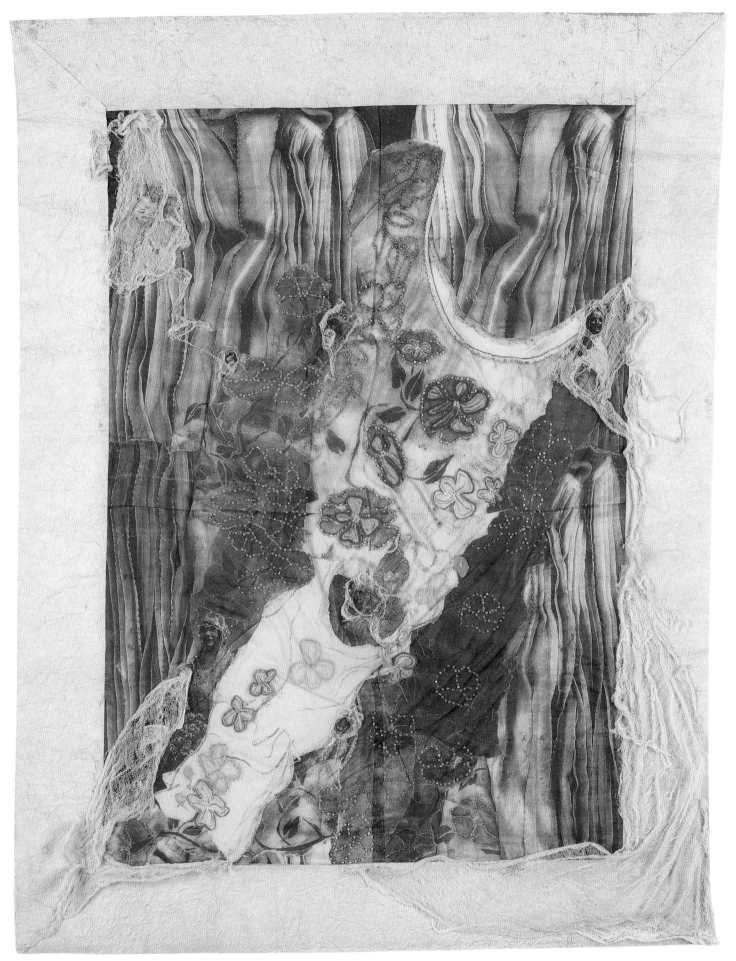

SIZE: 28 x 36½ INCHES (71 x 93 CM)

CONTEMPORARY ABSTRACT

THE POTENTIAL OF QUILTMAKING AS A MEANS OF EXPRESSION IS CONFIRMED BY THE ARRESTING, ABSTRACT IMAGES DISPLAYED IN THIS CHAPTER. SOME OF THESE QUILTS GIVE CLASSIC PATTERNS A CONTEMPORARY TWIST, WHILE OTHERS ABANDON TRADITION COMPLETELY TO CONVEY THE ARTIST'S PERSONAL VISION. ALL OF THESE QUILTS TEST THE BOUNDARIES OF FABRIC AND THREAD TO DELIVER VISUAL IMPACT AND TACTILE APPEAL. THE STRIKING DESIGNS INCLUDED HERE DEMONSTRATE THE DIVERSITY AND DEPTH OF THE FIBER MEDIUM.

BLACK MINUS BLACK

"I am trying to simplify the technical challenges of quilting and find more spontaneous ways to express myself in fabric. I most enjoy my work when I am not adhering to a rigid plan. I like to play with my fabrics, establish a dialogue with them, and let the design flow out. From a personal point of view, quilting is a valuable means of self-expression and discovery. Since I am not an especially vocal person, I ask my quilts to speak for me."

DIANA BUNNELL

The impact of this quilt is in the bold patterns created by discharge dyeing—removing color by treating various black fabrics with bleach. Different methods of applying the bleach were tried, including spraying, brushing, or folding and dipping the fabric into a bleach solution. The bleaching action was arrested by rinsing the fabric with water. Because the fabrics came from different manufacturers, the effects varied, with a range of colors resulting: white, pink, and peach; there was even a purplish cast on the black cotton canvas that was to be the background. Further design elements were added to the panels by stamping them with acrylic paint. Design decisions were made through trial arrangements on a vertical design wall. The pieces were then appliquéd onto a wholecloth of black cotton canvas. The rectangles were arranged on the backing in an indefinite grid to display the fabrics in a harmonious design.

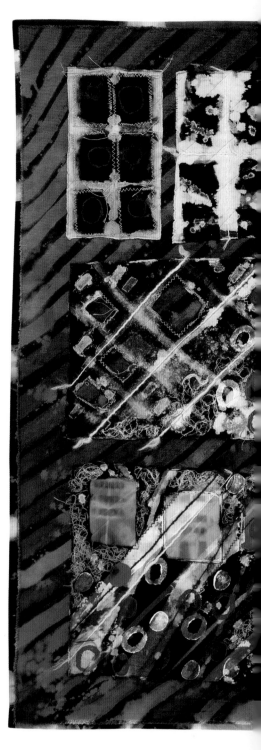

Overall design

Diana applied striking surface designs to several black fabrics using bleach discharge. The resulting panels of crosses, circles, and loose grids were assembled into a bold, abstract composition. Experimental effects were combined with a more controlled approach through the addition of stamped motifs and reverse appliqué.

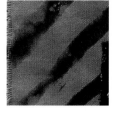

Wholecloth background

The wholecloth background was painted with bleach to produce a shadowy diagonal pattern.

Movement and energy

Both experimental and planned effects are combined in an energetic composition of simple recurring motifs such as circles, squares, and crosses. The diagonal lines in particular add movement and power, which is underlined by the raw textures and somber color palette.

SIZE: 51½ x 44 INCHES (130 x 112 CM)

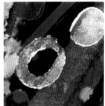

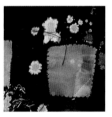

Printing with acrylic paint

Circular motifs stamped onto the surface with acrylic paint balance the three large rectangles appliquéd across the top of this panel. The addition of threads and yarns creates texture.

Appliqué

Six brown squares were appliquéd over this one particular panel, adding a degree of formality to the background textures.

SOHO SUNDAY

"I began quilting in earnest in the late 1960s, after making a quilt for my daughter using scraps left over from clothing I had made for her over the years. I am self-taught (by the blunder method!), but the example I had from my mother's originality and creativity let me know that any limitations were self-imposed. I enjoy all aspects of quiltmaking: it offers excitement when designing, accomplishment on completing the construction process, and meditative reflection during hand quilting. I still have more ideas than time and always want to know what will happen if …"

DIXIE HAYWOOD

An untitled, pencil, ink, and watercolor drawing by Vasily Kandinsky sparked Dixie's interest. The combination of a skewed grid, scattered graphic elements, and visual texture gave Dixie the idea of reinterpreting it in fabric. The grid was made by a foundation-piecing technique Dixie calls "same-fabric crazy piecing." The graphic detail—the part of the quilt most true to the watercolor—was the most interesting and challenging part of the process. Quilting was done "in the ditch" to reinforce the texture and the graphics. The combination of pastel and jewel colors with the fine graphics makes for a playful quilt, reinforced by the texture of fabric and thread.

Overall design

Fifty-four rhomboid shapes made from plain fabrics and set in an irregular grid form the structure of the quilt. Narrow black lines separate each of the units. Diagonal lines and fun graphic elements introduce movement and the rhythm of repetition.

Reverse appliqué with satin stitch

Dixie used reverse appliqué to create floating shapes in the center of a colored field. The edges of the fabric were decorated with machine satin stitching.

"Same-fabric crazy piecing"

Because of the asymmetrical grid, the entire quilt had to be blocked out full size on tracing paper, then each piece coded on the back for location and color. For each section, the same fabric was cut and re-cut as it was pieced onto the foundation. The changes in grain add subtle background texture to the linear design.

Color study

Dixie has used mostly pastels, but the inclusion of some darker colors adds zest to the palette. Black has a particular effect on the solid colors, making them more vibrant.

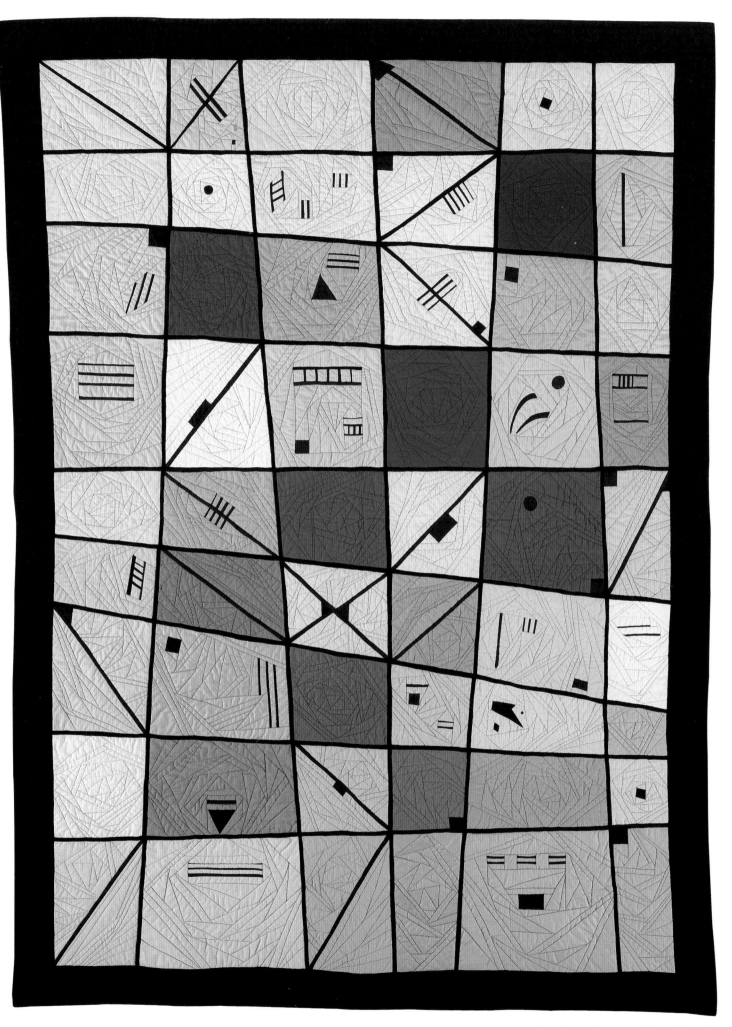

SIZE: 50 X 67 INCHES (127 X 170 CM)

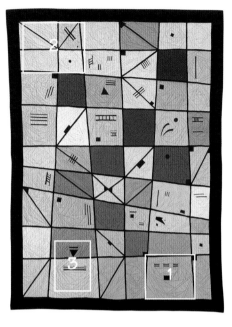

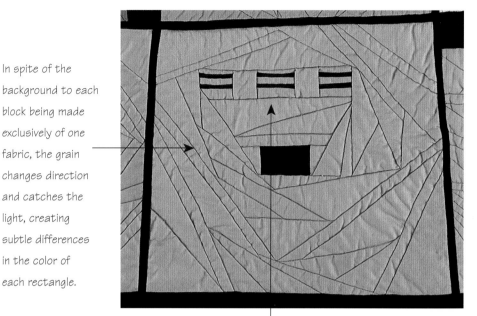

In spite of the background to each block being made exclusively of one fabric, the grain changes direction and catches the light, creating subtle differences in the color of each rectangle.

The quilt succeeds thanks to its combination of repetition and variety. Each of the black shapes and lines is carefully balanced and works with the colors to achieve a harmonious, abstract composition.

Every section is different and could stand as a distinct unit in its own right. As part of a collection, it intrigues us with its finely balanced lines, geometric elements, and pleasing patterns.

Detail 2: Construction of each unit

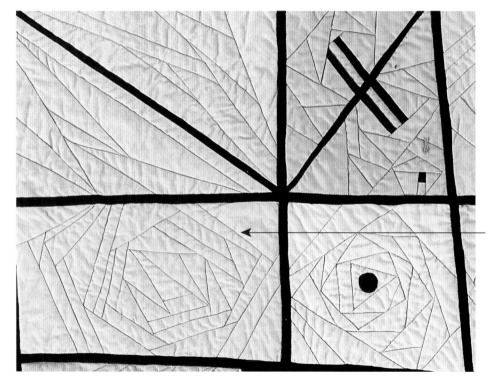

None of the blocks is a true square or rectangle, so, when under construction, care had to be taken not to reverse them or they would not have fit together. The plain, one-color blocks provide a resting place between the lively abstractions of the others.

When constructing the background blocks, patches were added randomly to the foundation, so there was no need to mark out the design first.

Detail 3: Crazy foundation piecing

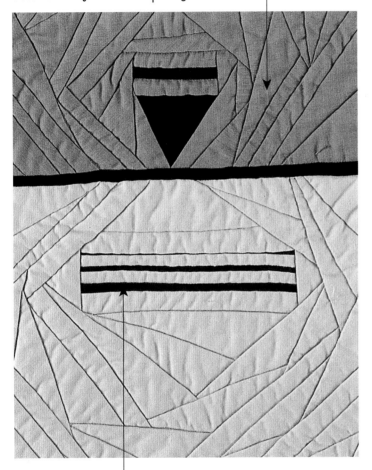

Some of the graphic details had to be pre-pieced before being incorporated into the crazy sections. The circles and a few other shapes were added to individual blocks with reverse appliqué after the relevant block had been pieced.

REVERSE APPLIQUÉ WITH MACHINED SATIN STITCH

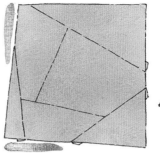

1 • Prepare the top layer. This could be a single piece of fabric or a piece of patchwork. If piecing onto a foundation, use a removable one such as Stitch-n-Tear.

2 • Make a template of the shape to be added. Select the appliqué fabric and cut a piece that is bigger than the shape by at least 1 inch (2.5 cm) all around.

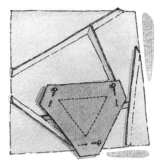

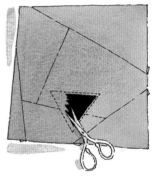

3 • Using a fabric marker, draw around the template on the top fabric to mark the appliqué position. Baste along the marked line to indicate the appliqué position on the reverse side. On the wrong side, pin the appliqué fabric over the basting stitches. Machine straight stitch around the shape.

4 • On the right side, use a small, sharp pair of scissors to cut away the top fabric, just inside the stitching line.

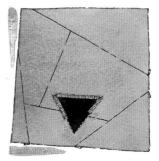

5 • Using a fabric stabilizer underneath to prevent the fabric from puckering, machine satin stitch over the straight stitching line, covering the raw edges of the top fabric. Trim the excess appliqué fabric from the back, close to the stitching.

FLAMBOYANT

"I grew up in South Africa where there was no tradition of quiltmaking. I taught myself paper template (English) piecing, then, after moving to Canada, I began to investigate American quiltmaking techniques. I enjoy the fact that the art of quilting is evolving—quiltmakers continue to invent new techniques and break rules in the creation of unique work—and that I am part of that exciting evolution. I also cherish the fact that the art of the needle is, in essence, the voice of women, and quilting has become a powerful medium for women to tell their stories."

VALERIE HEARDER

An exercise to make a design that could be repeated four times to make a spiral was the starting point for *Flamboyant*. Initially done as a woodblock print, Valerie realized it had the potential to be developed into a quilt. Striped and dotted taffeta was selected as the background for the four main blocks. The main, orange-yellow flame/flower motif has details such as veins, and flame or leaf shapes added to it. Ensuring the borders complemented the main flower shape was a challenge; the spiral, flowing movements of the central design continue into the border via quilting. The use of taffeta gives the quilt a rich surface reflection, adding to the impact of this striking design.

Overall design

The central flame/flower motif in hot, vibrant colors seems to shimmer in front of the darker background colors. The narrow sashing, which divides the four sections, emphasizes the repetition and clarifies the structure of the four blocks. The dynamic design, vibrant colors, and lustrous fabrics create a quilt full of impact.

Inspiration

The essence of the flaming red and orange blossoms of the South African Flamboyant tree and its likeness to fire are vividly captured in Valerie's quilt.

Techniques

A number of techniques were combined in the making of the quilt: fusible appliqué, hand appliqué, machine piecing, machine quilting, and hand stitching.

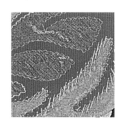

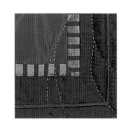

An "aura," or fiery halo, of gold mesh was fused into place around the tips of some of the smaller leaf shapes.

The main, larger shapes were simple, so Valerie added further elements such as the hand-stitched veins to embellish some of the edges.

Free-motion quilting in variegated metallic threads echoes the main shapes in the quilt and takes them into the borders.

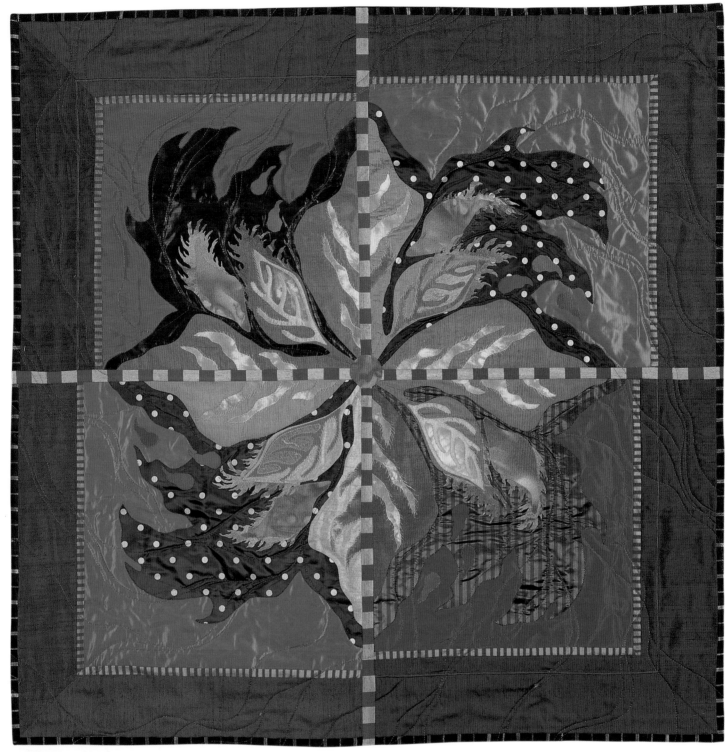

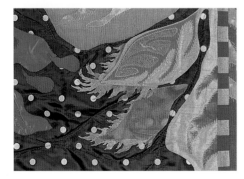

Block variations

Although the quilt is a four-block repeat, there are variations between the blocks to add interest to the quilt. The background fabric combinations differ in opposite blocks and the small details in the central section have slight variations in their treatment.

Four Broken Arms in One Year

"I began quiltmaking in my spare time in about 1976 when I worked as a dancer. When I retired from the stage, I studied textiles at Loughborough College of Art. I enjoy working with colors and enjoy seeing them bounce off each other. I have an extensive collection of fabrics and I usually use them in small pieces, strip pieced. As far as I am concerned an advantage of using the strip-piecing technique is that I can't always direct what part of a pattern will appear in which particular place within an arrangement. Consequently, there is an element of surprise in the piece."

BRIDGET INGRAM-BARTHOLOMÄUS

This quilt is a set of four separate panels which are stretched over wooden frames, and there are three different ways of arranging them for display. Initially, the design was done on a small scale. Then, when all the design decisions had been made, the pieces were drawn out full size. Templates were made from this full-size plan. As far as possible the strips were "mass produced," then the sections were cut out using the templates and stitched together. The quilting is all done on a sewing machine. The combination of graduated strips of color with the angular shapes are reminiscent of rock strata or sliced polished agate, and when viewing one arrangement of the panels in an exhibition, it is intriguing to imagine how the others would look.

Overall design

Making the quilt in four sections extends the options for different overall designs. Each unit is made up of angular sections of strips arranged in asymmetrical compositions. They are further linked by the fabrics and colors used.

Wedges

Bridget made strip-pieced units, graduating the values and strip widths, then cut and joined wedge-shaped pieces to make up the design for each panel. The direction of the strips changes to give the impression of angular facets, and the fabrics are carefully matched at the joins to preserve continuity. It is possible to identify the wedge-shaped sections by the changes in direction of the lines.

Inspiration

Although the quilt takes its name from the fact that four broken arms were suffered by members of Bridget's family within one year, the influence of rock strata is obvious.

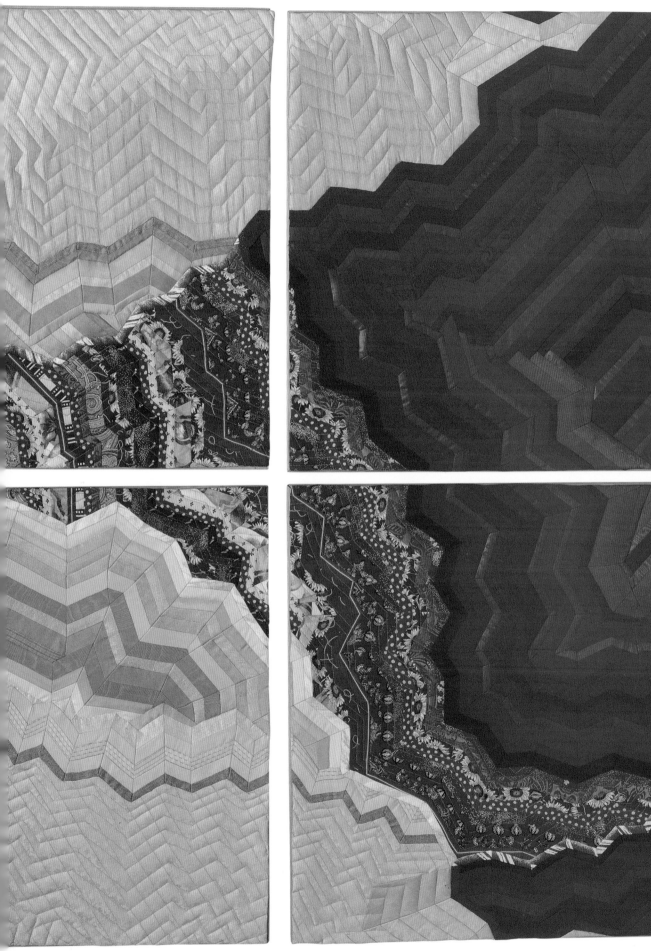

SIZE OF EACH PANEL: 24 x 24 INCHES (61 x 61 CM)

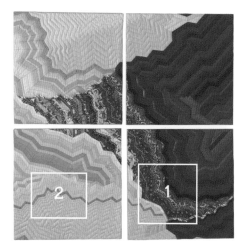

The use of patterned fabrics in a variety of different scales, but always containing both red and yellow, makes a balanced transition between the plain red and yellow fabrics.

Details are selected to highlight the effects that are realized by the combined choice of fabrics, methods of construction, and the quilting—all of which work together to create four original panels.

In the areas where plain fabric was used, the variation in the widths of the strips is more visible. Where patterned fabrics were used, the strips are less clearly defined.

Detail 2: Surface texture

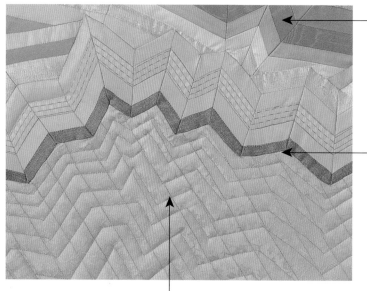

Quilting is much more visible on the light areas of the quilt, the solid fabric reflecting the bas-relief of the stitches.

The machine quilting follows the lines created by the strips and sections, emphasizing the angles of the design.

High and low contrast is used between the fabric strips to create both impact and subtlety in the plain areas.

Constructing the quilt in four separate but related units made it possible to arrange them in different ways. This piece was made for one of a series of exhibitions by the Quilt Art organization—a group of quiltmakers who wish to promote contemporary quiltmaking as an innovative craft, with the intention of changing the concept of quilts from functional articles to works of art in which content and visual impact predominate. Bridget comments, "I found it quite compelling to make, and was extremely pleased when the three different hanging variations did work out, not just in theory but also in practice."

Arrangement 1: In this arrangement the plain cream fabric provides restful background areas, which project the darker yellow, red, and patterned areas into the foreground as the main composition.

Arrangement 2: Here, the lighter areas become the main focus of the composition, silhouetted against the darker fabrics, which provide a rich backdrop full of movement and visual texture.

Arrangement 3: When the panels are displayed side by side as in this arrangement, the linear apects of the design are highlighted and the pattern's similarity to rock strata becomes even more apparent.

ROSE TRELLIS

"The design for Rose Trellis was developed as a result of experimenting with Crazy Log Cabin designs. I wanted a complex design that would challenge my piecing skills but not require large quantities of any one color. I worked from the center of each block outward, selecting the colors as I went. If I ran out of any particular color I either changed it completely or used the nearest that was available. I had no idea how it would look when it was finished."

IRENE MACWILLIAM

Many quilters, having gained expertise in the usual skills of piecing and quilting, set themselves more complex challenges. By scaling the blocks down to 4 inch (10 cm) squares, each of which has 31 pieces of fabric, Irene certainly gave herself problems to solve. The technique of foundation or paper piecing makes it easier to use tiny pieces of fabric, but great skill is still required to fit them all together accurately, so that matching points fit exactly. Here, there are 36 blocks in solid, bright colors. In each set of four, blocks are turned to form mirror images so that the triangles at the corners of each block combine to make diamond and star shapes. Tiny folded strips of blue define some of the outer shapes of each block, giving even more impact to the diamonds and stars that intersect the quilt. A kaleidoscopic design of dazzling complexity results.

Overall design

A complex overall design is created by placing blocks edge to edge. Numerous secondary designs appear, and it takes 16 to fully exploit the potential. The single block disappears, merging to create a design full of fascinating repetition. The colors change their position within the blocks from the center to the border, adding to the visual impact.

Quilting

Machine quilting outlines the shapes created by combining blocks.

Folded strip inserts

Folded strips inserted between some of the outer segments define the star and diamond shapes more clearly.

With the creation of sharper points, the use of smaller pieces of fabric, and the stitching of tinier, more even stitches, Irene has managed to incorporate as much detail and interest in this small quilt as might be found in a full-size one. She has successfully exploited appropriate techniques, such as foundation piecing and machine quilting, to achieve her objectives.

A lightweight muslin or sew-in Vilene will add a little extra weight to the quilt when foundation piecing. However, Irene preferred to use a removable paper-based foundation that was torn away after use, adding no weight.

Detail 1: Foundation piecing

Foundation piecing is the only way such small pieces of fabric could be made to fit accurately together. By stitching the patches to a predrawn foundation it is possible to work on a small scale. Nevertheless stitching the blocks together still presents a considerable challenge.

Detail 2: Quilting

The quilting was done with a smaller than regular stitch, with the feed dogs engaged and with a walking foot, in straight lines, to echo the geometric design.

Machine quilting is used to outline the shapes created between the blocks. It is easier to match the small scale of the piece with machine stitches than with quilting by hand.

Detail 3: Color placement

The blocks are not all identical in coloring but the color placement is symmetrical. This adds to the complexity and maintains interest when viewing the quilt.

Alternative block settings

By altering the orientation of the blocks and changing the colors, a completely different effect results.

Example 1

The block is quarter turned in sequence resulting in a different design. Irene picked the most effective arrangement of the blocks for her quilt by using mirror images to match side points creating secondary designs between the blocks.

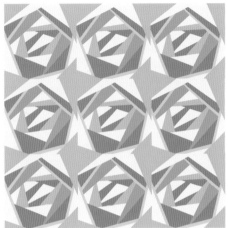

Example 2

In this example the orientation of the block is consistently the same. A repeat design is the result, but points at the edges do not match up as they do when the block is flipped and turned.

CRAZY LOG CABIN BLOCK

1 • Single block
Crazy Log Cabin block, so called because it is worked from the center outward in the manner of Log Cabin blocks but with asymmetrical shapes.

2 • One set of four blocks
Each block is quarter turned and flipped over to create a mirror image. The triangles that cut across the corners come together to form a diamond.

3 • Another set of four blocks
A different arrangement of the same four blocks makes yet another design.

QUILT FOR A HOT NIGHT

"One of the challenges in today's world is to make time to let the imagination flow. I liken it to lying on your back watching the clouds go by and finding shapes within. So, when I can't sleep I play the imagining or possibility game. This quilt is the result of such a night that was hot and humid. The question arose— how to make a quilt for such a night? The randomly strip-pieced lengths are joined with rouleau strips, not only to let in the air but to add to the shadows of the night."

ROSEMARY PENFOLD

Five long strips of multicolored, solid and print fabrics were pieced together and bound. The strips, created from random widths of fabric, are reminiscent of early scrap quilts, in which speed and utility were the motivation for inventiveness. Working within the rich tradition of quilting as an expressive medium, Rosemary moved into the contemporary arena of the art quilt by using the innovative technique of joining fabric strips with a ladder of black rouleau strips. The function of the quilt is illustrated in the title, but it is evident that this quilt is intended for the wall, thereby combining the established motives for quiltmaking—practical and decorative. Simple techniques have been manipulated to create a sophisticated piece of work, with humor, originality, and an exuberant color scheme.

Overall design

The quilt is machine pieced from randomly cut fabrics, creating five long, multicolored strips of bright prints and solids. The strips are edged with black binding and joined with black rouleau strips every 3 to 4 inches (8 to 10 cm), approximately 3 inches (8 cm) apart. There is a broader black border at the top and bottom.

Fabrics

Bold, high-contrast fabrics in large-scale prints, like the black-and-white stripes and dots, are teamed with bright colors and patterns in a mixture of scales. Organization of the fabrics is random and this makes it rewarding viewing, both from a distance and close up.

Rouleau strips

Rouleau strips are narrow strips of fabric with neatened edges. They connect the five long strips of the quilt and create their own pattern as they repeat across the gaps in a rather irregular way, casting shadows.

Cohesive design

The use of black for the binding, the connecting strips, and the top and bottom borders unify the assortment of brightly colored fabrics used in the long strips, creating a composite whole from disparate elements.

The patchwork lengths

The patchwork lengths are of slightly irregular widths, but this reflects the random nature of the fabric arrangement and the crazy ladder formed by the joining strips.

Quilting

Quilting was done by hand using a thicker than usual thread—Perlé Cotton number 8—to add yet more texture to the surface of the quilt.

SIZE: 37 X 72½ INCHES
(94 X 184 CM)

SCATTERED LASERS

"Classes taken with Nancy Crow and Aartha Greep gave me the courage to try out experimental techniques. I began by making a waistcoat, but when I was asked to teach these skills I felt that I needed another example. An intense few days of layering, cutting, and shuffling fabrics, and inserting strips followed and the quilt top was finished. There was no pre-planning other than the fabric selection, which was made for maximum impact: a range of grays, enlivened with high-contrast black-and-white stripes and checks, and multicolored florals."

HILARY RICHARDSON

The method of construction for this quilt—cutting layered fabrics, then reassembling them—created four similar, but not identical, center blocks, which were arranged in quarter turns. The resulting composition is full of interest, holding the eye and keeping it moving over the surface of the quilt. The outer border continues the shapes used in the center blocks, and a narrow inner border of high contrast black and white striped fabric separates the different sections of the quilt. The changes of direction in the piecing and the narrow bands of vibrant fabrics combine to make a dynamic quilt that illustrates its title. The surface texture created by the overlaid sheer fabrics, machine embroidery, and free-motion machine quilting enhance the design.

Overall design

The center of the quilt is composed of four quarter sections of repeated angular shapes. The activity in the center section gives an appearance of intensification. The inner striped border contains this activity, while the outer border acts as a calming frame.

Value

Three values of gray form a mono-chromatic yet varied background that allows the bright reds, yellows, and floral prints to shine.

DIRECT LAYERING, CUTTING, AND PIECING

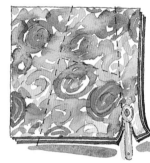

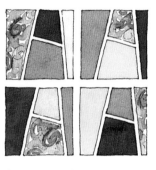

1 • Cut up to eight squares of fabric 1½ to 2 inches (4 to 5 cm) larger than the desired finished blocks. Layer the fabrics right sides up, and press the stack together with an iron. Cut the stacked squares into four or more shapes with a rotary cutter.

2 • Separate the pieces and reassemble them into squares, mixing the fabrics.

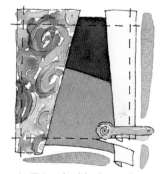

3 • Stitch the pieces together, using a scant ¼ inch (0.75 cm) seam allowance. The edges won't fit together exactly, but this doesn't matter.

4 • Trim the blocks to the desired shape and size.

SIZE: 40 x 40 INCHES (102 x 102 CM)

Embellishment

Embroidery with multicolored threads is used in the center and to extend the pieced lines of the quilt into the outer borders.

Overlaying

Voile and net are used on the borders—overlaid in shapes that correspond with those in the blocks in the center of the quilt.

Piped edges

The outer edges of the quilt are piped, giving it a crisp, clearly defined outer line that contains the design.

30 CIRCLES

"I realized that quiltmaking was the natural melding of my two strengths and passions— graphics and textiles—after visiting the Art Quilt exhibition Visions *in San Diego in 1996. I knew then that quilting was the natural medium for my artistic voice. Fabric and thread appeal to me more than paint because of their flexibility, texture, and movement. With these as my mediums, I have merged my love of fabric, color, and graphic design into what is becoming accepted in the art world as Art Quilts."*

CAROL SCHEPPS

Circles, a universal symbol of eternity and health, are represented in this colorful piece of work. Four different sized circles sit within squares of fabric arranged in a grid. The circles are randomly cut, giving a feeling of movement and spontaneity. Surface embellishments provide interest and color contrast. The idea was developed when Carol observed the way the colors in random piles of fabric on her worktable played off each other and she began to shift them into different groupings. She comments, "one thing led to another and I cut a few circles… When they are stacked up ready to be quilted, each one revealed a wonderful surprise." There is a colorful intensity in each composition of circles, and as they react together the visual impact is magnified to produce a dazzling effect.

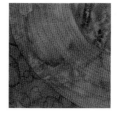

Overall design

A series of 30 different colored squares, each containing a composition of four circles, provides the background. The circles were cut freehand then placed on top of each other. The composition and color combination of each set is different. The regular arrangement of the background squares provides a formal element, which gives structure to the spontaneity of the circle compositions.

Construction of the circles

The circles were fused to each other, then fused to the background fabric. Each one takes on a unique personality as a result of the combinations of colors and textures.

Quilting

Machine quilting follows the contours of the circles, using threads that blend and contrast to provide additional color details.

Background squares

The background squares, arranged in a grid of dark colors, provide a foil to the exuberance of the circles appliquéd onto the surface.

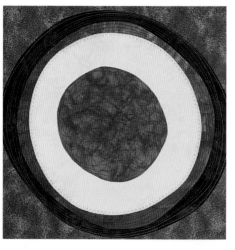

Color study

Yellow is a key color and provides sparkle. The yellow areas are strategically balanced, disturbing the symmetry of the background grid and drawing the eye across the surface.

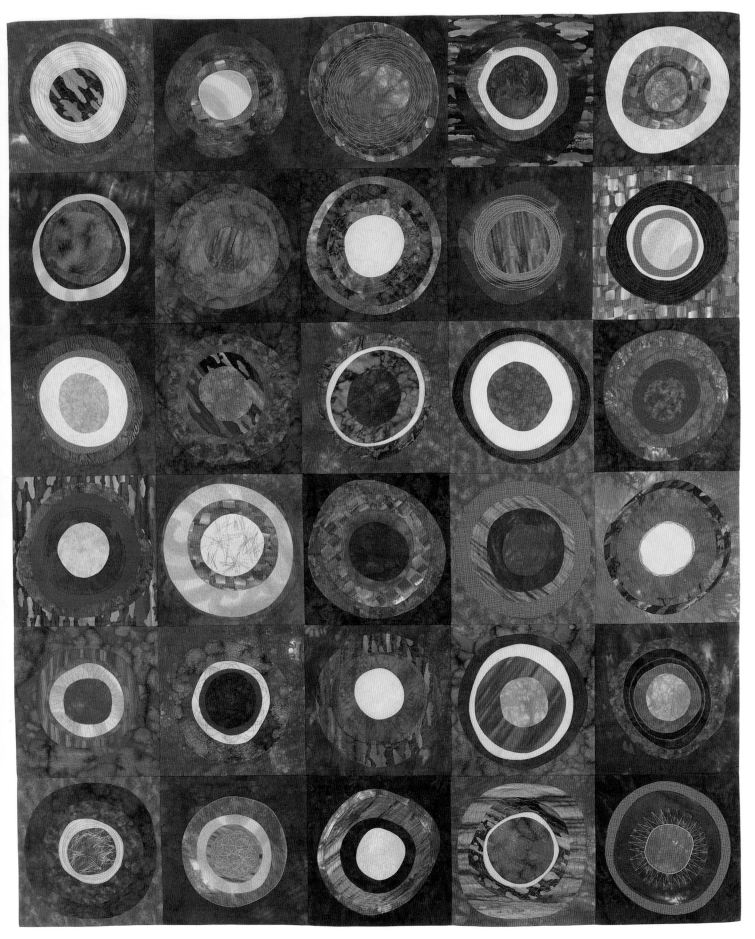

SPINNER HIT FOR SIX

"In 1998 I started to investigate kaleidoscopic designs. At the same time I was designing a quilt for an exhibition on the theme of cricket at Lord's cricket ground in London. The movement of the spin bowler and ball provided the starting point for this quilt, and the six equilateral triangle segments which form it link with the cricket term 'hit for six.' I drew out one equilateral triangle to be repeated six times to make the design. Curves inside the triangle, and Flying Geese triangles inside the curves, create lots of movement. I love the 'order and method' aspect of seams that fit and points that meet, and offsetting these with the spontaneity of my color choices."

ANJA TOWNROW

The impression of spinning movement, created by the curves and spirals, is complemented by the bold use of bright colors. Meanwhile, all the separate components of the quilt are balanced, and the resulting whole is contained by the striped fabric borders. The construction of such a quilt presents technical difficulties: curved seams require a degree of skill, but the ultimate achievement is more in the fact that on viewing the quilt it is the success of the overall design, and not questions of technique, that we are aware of.

Overall design

The initial impact of the curved Flying Geese segments is underlined by other impressions of circular movement. The large circular motifs set at each angle of the quilt and the small ones that are randomly placed, all add to the effect of movement. The colorful intensity of the fabrics adds to the excitement of the composition.

Foundation piecing

Anja pieced her design on a paper foundation to accurately join the asymmetrical triangles in the curved Flying Geese strips.

Reverse appliqué

After joining the six pieced triangles that form the quilt, Anja used metallic thread to appliqué the large spirals. Orange fabric was placed underneath them to give the spirals more definition.

SIZE: 70 X 60 INCHES (178 X 152 CM)

Broderie perse

This is a method of cutting out motifs from a fabric and appliquéing them to the background. Here, small spirals cut from printed fabric were added randomly to the composition.

Quilting

The three layers of the quilt were first stitched "in the ditch" (along the seam lines) to secure them together, then Anja embellished the surface with decorative quilting, using both variegated metallic and invisible monofilament thread with a walking foot.

REVERSE APPLIQUÉ SPIRALS

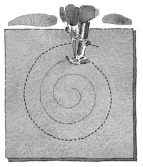

1 • Place one piece of fabric on top of another with right sides uppermost. Press them together. Pencil a spiral motif onto the fabric. Stitch along the pencil line, working inward from the outer edge. Stitching lines should be ½ inch (1.5 cm) apart.

2 • Cut a narrow channel between the stitching lines and around the outer circle of stitching.

3 • Brush the top fabric with a dry nailbrush to fray the raw edges. Reverse-appliqué spirals can be made in any size and either pieced into a quilt top or appliquéd onto it.

BIG SKY 4: LANDINGS

"This piece is the fourth in a series that features a value gradient—graduated shades—of hand-dyed 'sky' fabrics purchased from Stacy Michell of 'Shades.' The quilting is an evolved form of hand quilting termed 'bigstitching,' developed from studying sources which include Japanese sashiko and Welsh utility quilts. The value gradient, flowing in opposing directions, reflects the adverse forces that drive us all—and the equilibrium that lies somewhere in between."

JO WALTERS

In this tongue-in-cheek interpretation of a U.F.O. theme, the traditional Birds in the Air block has been incorporated into a bar setting. The block bars are separated by broad strips of graduated sky fabric, which has been further modified by overpainting to achieve the desired effect. Colors graduate in opposite directions along the vertical in a limited color palette ranging from gold to blue-gray. Jo studied a number of styles in order to develop her hand quilting methods, with the intention of maximizing the design impact of her stitches, and speeding the process by using bigger stitches and thicker threads. In the pieced columns the quilting stitches follow the contours of the patchwork, while in the alternating bars a number of freely drawn designs, developed from traditional Welsh and North Country quilts, add coordinating colors and intriguing texture.

Inspiration

Montana is known as Big Sky Country. This nickname was one of the factors in the creation of the Big Sky series because Jo "has fantasies of living in such a place one day."

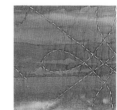

Fabric dyeing

The sky fabrics were painted, overdyed, and discharged in order to achieve a smooth gradation in shades and depict realistic skyscapes.

Overall design

Four columns of traditional Birds in the Air block were set on point within broad bars of fabric that graduate from light to dark. The quilting designs follow the strippy format, occasionally overlapping the divisions between the strips.

Quilting

Quilting patterns were bigstitched in Welsh Laurel, North Country, and freehand drawn cables. Six different colors of thread were used.

Pieced block

A version of the traditional Birds in the Air block was set on point and appears to be descending in columns of light.

SIZE: 62 X 63 INCHES (157 X 160 CM)

KINDRED SPIRITS 1–5

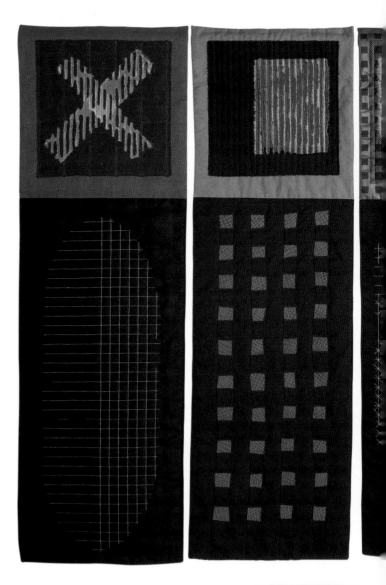

"I saw my first quilt at the age of 16 on a trip to America. I was fascinated by what could be done with fabrics, combining colors, and the textures that could be created in quilting. When I started to make quilts myself I knew that something exciting was happening in the U.S.A., and that this was a medium suitable for creating pictures. There is always a new challenge in the process of making quilts and it is always a special feeling to have the visible, finished product in my hands."

CHARLOTTE YDE

Kindred Spirits is part of an ongoing series of long, narrow, panels in which experimental techniques such as free-cut piecing, layering, slashing, and cutting are combined with machine and hand quilting. The series is based on the idea of things having similarities but retaining individuality. The first, entitled *Personalities 1–4*, won First Prize in the first European Quilt Triennial. Charlotte uses abstract symbolism to interpret her ideas. Regular grids and patterns combine with more organic shapes and textures in a limited palette of red, black, gray, and gold. Each of the component parts follows a similar format: a single figure at the top of each panel is divided from the base, yet each element contains some form of rhythmic repetition. Each one is different however, helping to sustain interest in the collection as a whole.

Overall design

Each of the five separate, abstract panels could stand alone, but when looking at the collection the viewers are struck by both the similarities and differences. Repetition of simple shapes such as crosses and grids is supplemented by more organic motifs reminiscent of cloud formations or waves. Machine quilting has been combined with hand quilting, and the relief effect of quilting is another important aspect of Charlotte's quilts.

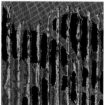

Layering/slashing

The tops of the narrow panels were layered and slashed. Layers of fabric were stacked together, stitched so that channels formed, and then cut to reveal the colors underneath.

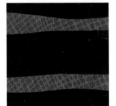

Free-form piecing

Slight curves were
introduced into the
pieced panels by
overlapping edges
that were stitched
together and cut
through at the
same time to make
a perfect match.

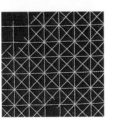

Quilting

The quilted grids
were machine
stitched from the
back with a thick,
white thread in the
bobbin to make
the quilting more
decorative.

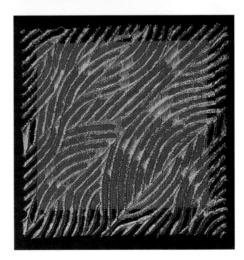

Color study

A limited palette of colors unifies the
variety of marks and patterns. Black and
red form a counterpoint, with additional
details added in gray, white, and gold.

SIZE: FOUR PANELS 14
INCHES WIDE AND
ONE PANEL 47 INCHES
WIDE, ALL PANELS 45
INCHES LONG (36 AND
120 X 114 CM)

TEXTURED AND EMBELLISHED

❖

THE TACTILE NATURE OF FIBER ART, WHICH ADDS SO MUCH TO THE ALLURE OF QUILTS, IS EXPLORED IN THIS CHAPTER. INNOVATIVE FABRIC MANIPULATION TECHNIQUES, SUCH AS ORIGAMI FOLDS AND FRAYED APPLIQUÉ, COMBINE WITH DECORATIVE DYEING, PAINTING, PRINTING, AND EMBROIDERY TO PRODUCE IRRESISTIBLE SURFACE APPEAL. BLURRING THE DISTINCTIONS BETWEEN QUILTING AND EMBROIDERY, WEAVING AND PIECING, THESE QUILTS REPRESENT THE CURRENT TREND TOWARD ABUNDANT TEXTURE AND EMBELLISHMENT IN THE ART QUILT.

ARIZONA MOUNTAINS

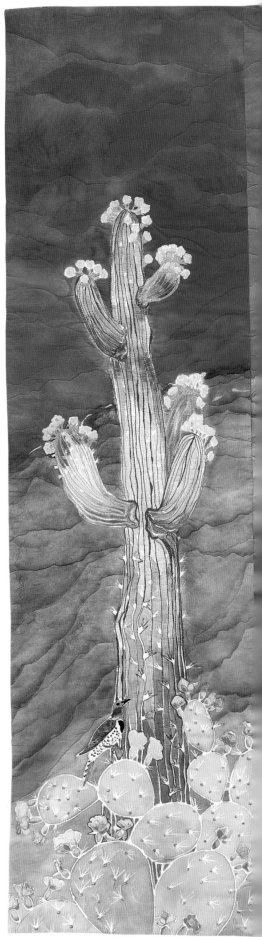

"My quilts bring together a love of art, fabric, and nature. A spring trip to the mountains and deserts of Arizona was the inspiration behind this piece. I was delighted to see so many cacti and wildflowers in bloom. The land was alive with birds, but it was the Gila woodpecker that I found most attractive. The beautiful red rock in various formations was so captivating that I found myself just gazing out into the mountains."

GINNY ECKLEY

Over the years Ginny has developed her own techniques for creating unique textile art. She combines the fine art skill of painting with experimental surface design on silk. The mountain backdrop was created in stages: a 23mm silk crepe was chosen to create the soft, pebbly texture of the mountains, and their soft color was produced by several reddish brown washes. The fissures in the rock face were added by airbrushing against the edges of torn cardboard. To achieve the darker base of the rock, the back of the silk was painted with black Colorhue dye over plastic. The silk picked up the creases in the plastic, creating angular lines. Since the first layer was a transparent wash, the black showed through. To create the impression of distance, a border on the left-hand side and across the base forms the foreground and contains more detail and brighter colors.

Overall design

By combining techniques and materials in innovative ways a realistic depiction of a timeless mountain landscape has been created. Details of flowers and foliage in the foreground frame the main composition—the grand backdrop of the mountains.

The cactus

The cactus stands in profile against a deep blue sky, forming the focus of the foreground, drawing the eye, and providing interest with details such as the birds hidden in the foliage.

Contrast between the fine details in the borders and the irregular texture of the mountain are examined in these enlarged areas of the quilt.

Airbrush and stencil technique were used to add detail to the color-washed background.

Detail 1: Color study

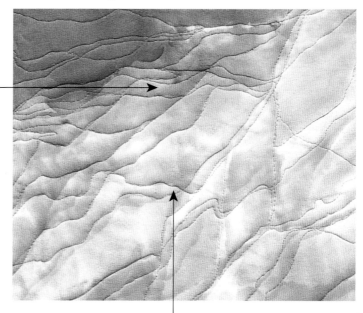

The limited palette of earth colors in the mountain is offset by realistic flowers and vegetation in lighter yellows and red in the bottom and in the left-hand border.

Detail 2: Fabric painting

A unique quality of silk painting is the luminescent colors that arise from the sheen of the silk.

The sharp thorns of the cactus were drawn with fabric markers and Lumière paint.

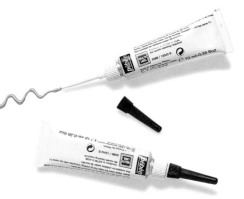

Gutta

Gutta was used to create a resist that prevented the colors from running together. Any breaks in the resist line allowed colors to bleed from one area to another. Gutta can be transparent, colored, or metallic, and forms a characteristic element of a design. Water-based gutta can be washed out with cold water.

Detail 3: The foreground

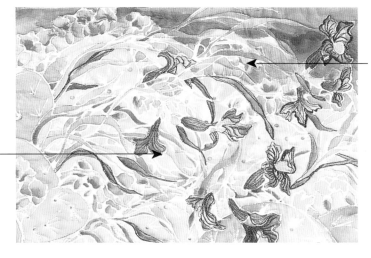

Once the foreground flowers had been drawn onto the silk, Ginny outlined the shapes with a water-soluble resist, using a fine-tipped applicator to define them. Then she painted the flowers with Setacolor silk paint. Embroidery in bright silk threads was used to add further details.

The scale and detail in the foreground create an illusion of distance in the rest of the picture, giving the mountains a monumental quality.

PAINTING ON SILK

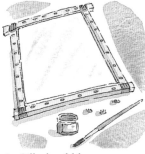 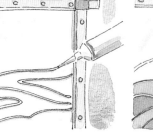 

1 • Silk should be prewashed before it is painted. There are a number of different types of silk, in varying weights and textures. The one you use will affect the result. Stretch the silk taut in an embroidery hoop or stretcher frame. Choose a water-based paint from a brand that has inter-mixable colors and can be fixed using a hot iron.

2 • Use gutta to draw the outline of the design onto the silk—use the applicator attached to the container or a paint brush. The line should be even and continuous. Allow to dry.

3 • Mix the paint colors on a palette, or use pure, unmixed paints. Touch the center of an area surrounded by gutta so that the paint floods to the line.

4 • When the dye has dried, fix the colors by ironing the silk on the reverse side for two minutes at the cotton heat setting. Keep the iron moving all the time.

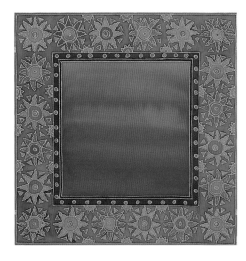

Silk painting

Silk painting techniques are ideal for experimentation. The vibrant colors of the paints combine with the sheen of the silk to create a characteristic brilliance. For a softer look, dampen the silk with a mist spray before painting. A mottled effect can be achieved by sprinkling salt crystals onto the surface of the damp paint before it is dry. Wash out the salt residue under cold water after fixing. Finally, try mixing the colors on the silk surface.

Ikat Quilt/Rhythm II

"As a German quiltmaker I enjoy a lot of freedom. In Germany only a few people are interested in quilts and there are no limits imposed by tradition. I learned the techniques of quiltmaking gradually, and by trial and error. From the beginning I have dyed all my own fabric. Some years ago I realized the potential for the 'wrong side' of the quilt—that visible seams and invisible quilting create a three-dimensional surface. This is the second in a series of three quilts."

Inge Hueber

Inge Hueber is a founding member of Quilt Art, a group of selected quiltmakers who work to achieve a new acceptance for an old medium—to raise the status of quilts from domestic articles to contemporary art. *Ikat Quilt/Rhythm II* makes reference to another textile technique: decorative weaving, in which patterns are bound and dyed into the warp threads before they are woven. This gives ikat designs a characteristic soft-edged look. Here, a complex pattern evolves out of 11 strips in a rainbow of colors. The pattern is visible, but also fluid and light, taking on the characteristics of ikat weaving by blurring the hard-edged color divisions. Inge comments, "I enjoy the contrast between a rigid concept and a floating result, on the one side a quilt is a technical object and needs serious craftsmanship, on the other side it is about the expression of feelings."

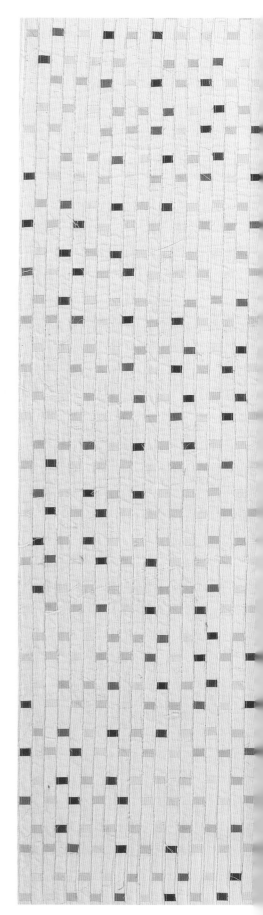

Overall design
The quilt gives credit to the technique of ikat weaving; although there is a repeated sequence of colored squares interwoven with the cream background, there is a slight shift in the repetition. Interest is maintained as the eye tries to establish pattern sequences and order. Surface texture created by raw-edge seams adds to the complexity. Sustained viewing is rewarded with an appreciation of the complex design.

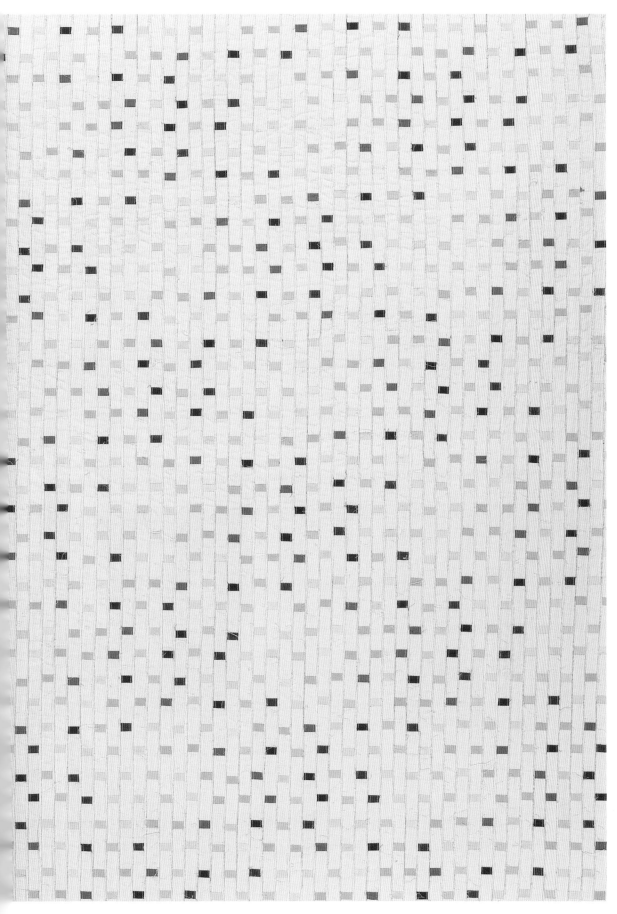

Working method

Inge works directly with the fabric rather than with an initial drawing. "I construct and think in my head before I cut the cloth, then I am just curious how the idea will work in reality," she says.

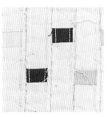

Red fabric

The red fabric is the key factor in the design because it is the most visible to the eye and, therefore, creates a pattern for the viewer.

SIZE: 79 X 78 INCHES (201 X 198 CM)

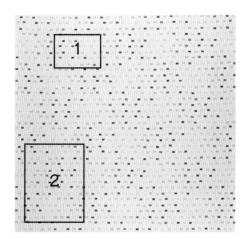

Detail 1: Quilting

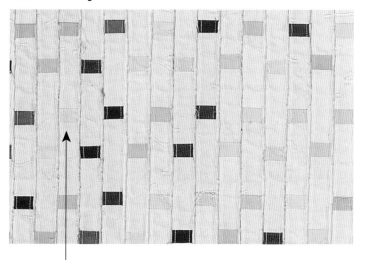

An appreciation of the composition of Inge's quilt and her working methods is enhanced by closer examination. The initial impact of the design is complemented by the tactile quality produced by the piecing and quilting.

Inge reverses the usual trend of invisible seams and visible quilting. In her work, it is important that the seams are visible and that the machine quilting becomes invisible.

Detail 2: Strip piecing

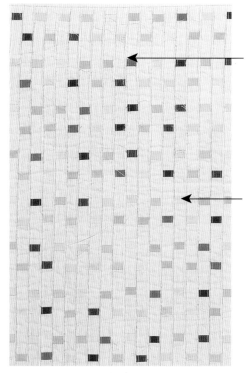

After piecing the strips together, sections of the quilt were laid out for consideration before final decisions about the composition were made. The relative positions of the colored squares, and the patterns they make, determined the basis of the design.

The pattern is the result of the color repetition and the equal widths of the cream and colored strips. Precision and care were vital, both when cutting the strips and in stitching them back together, to keep the pattern regular.

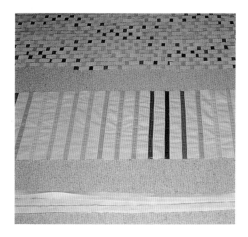

Work in progress

A series of 11 narrow strips, each one a different color and separated by a broader cream strip, were stitched together in a repetitive order. The strip-pieced units were then cut into squares and shifted slightly before being reassembled.

HAND-DYEING FABRIC

If you are looking for a specific color of fabric that is not commercially available, or a two-color effect, the solution may be to dye your own. You can also experiment with simple patterns made using resist techniques.

For hand-dyeing you will need the following equipment: shallow plastic containers such as large ice cream cartons, plastic bottles, measuring jugs, preserve jars, cups, and spoons. Reserve all equipment for dyeing only, since the chemicals may contaminate food. Other requirements: household salt, soda ash, running water and a sink, an additive-free soap such as Synthrapol, rubber gloves, and dust mask.

1 • To plain-dye a fabric, mix dye solution according to the manufacturer's instructions, wet the fabric, and then immerse it in the dye solution. If an even, allover color is required, the fabric must be kept moving by agitating the liquid. For small pieces of fabric, fill a strong, resealable plastic bag with dye solution, place the fabrics in the bag, and seal. The fabrics can then be agitated without any spillage. Follow the manufacturer's instructions to fix and rinse the dye.

2 • To use multiple dye colors, place the wet fabric in a shallow container, then spoon two or more dye colors over it. To prevent the colors from merging too much, do not touch the fabrics for the requisite time, then fix and rinse. If colors appear too strong they can be diluted.

3 • Patterns can be introduced into the fabrics by using various resist methods. Tie knots in the fabric, or tie small pebbles into it with fine string before dyeing. Gather the fabric with running stitches pulled up to pleat it, or bind the fabric at intervals. The pattern of the stitches or string will show where it has resisted the dye. If you are not happy with the first effects, overdye the result with another color.

Dyes. Cold water, fiber-reactive dyes, which produce pure, bright colors, are available in craft and art-supply shops, or there are mail order firms which specialize in supplying them. Whatever your choice, they will be accompanied by instructions on how to use them.
Fabrics. Different fibers will react differently to the dyes, so experiment with a variety of fabrics. One-hundred percent bleached or unbleached cotton is a good choice to begin with. Printed fabrics can also be overdyed to change the colors. Wash all fabrics before dyeing. Half- or quarter-yard cuts are ideal.

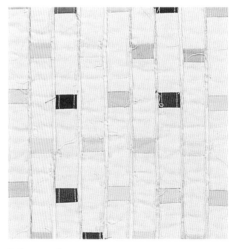

Color study

Inge used gradation dyeing to achieve smooth color runs, which involved precise measuring and dilution of the dye solutions.

STONE'S THROW

"The pleasure of putting together different fabrics to create a new design motivates me to make quilts. I enjoy all aspects of the craft: both hand and machine work—but I particularly enjoy seeing the finished quilt emerge from the thousands of tiny design decisions involved in the making process. I work with the fabrics directly on a vertical design wall, from a basic idea in my head, which often changes and develops as the quilt takes shape."

SARA IMPEY

Cathedral Window is a technique of folding one fabric to provide a window to showcase small diamonds of contrasting fabrics. In this quilt Sarah abandoned the traditional grid format and found a new freedom by appliquéing the units to the background. The type of Cathedral Window units featured are a variation on the basic one known as Secret Garden. The fabric used for the pieced background is cotton lawn, which Sara first scrunch-dyed to produce a textured effect. Fabrics for the individual Secret Garden patches were speckle-dyed by sprinkling dry dye powder over wet fabric. The colors change from glowing yellows to a range of blues, giving an impression of ripples. The radiating lines give the quilt depth and create a perfect balance with the subtle changes of color in the hand-dyed fabrics.

Overall design

Superimposed as a secondary design on the top layer, the appliquéd units radiate from a point that is slightly off-center. The center point draws the eye at first, but then the attention of the viewer is caught by the balance between the radiating lines and the circles that spread out from the luminous center point.

Inspiration

Weathered lichen on stone inspired the design and colors of this quilt, which is one of a series using these colors.

Quilt center

This detail of the center of the quilt's large circle clearly shows the precise positioning of the Cathedral Window units and the subtle gradation of color in the hand-dyed fabrics.

Size: 54 x 66 inches (137 x 167 cm)

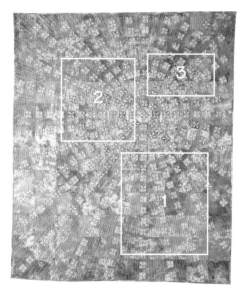

Areas of interest showing more detail include the pieced background, the Secret Garden units, the quilting, and the delicate effects of texture and gradual color change in the hand-dyed fabrics.

The background is machine pieced in 6 inch (15 cm) squares. The scrunch-dyeing of the background contrasts with the speckle-dyeing of the appliquéd units.

The subtle color variations that occur with these hand-dyeing methods are emphasized by the folding and stitching employed to make the Secret Garden units.

Detail 2: Hand quilting

Sara hand quilted around each patch, then added lines radiating from the center between each patch as they spread out.

Hand and machine stitching.
Apart from the machine-pieced background and some stitching on the binding, the whole quilt is sewn by hand.

VARIATIONS ON CATHEDRAL WINDOW

The base squares made for Cathedral Window designs can be folded in various ways. In these two blocks, the contrasting fabric used in the traditional version is omitted. The decorative element is provided by the folded fabric.

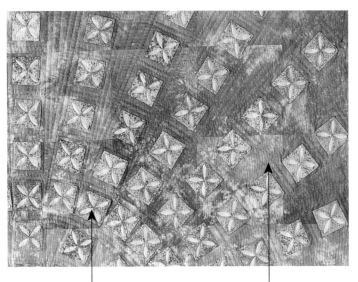

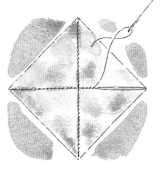
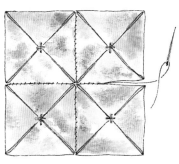

1 • Make up four Cathedral Window units to the stage where the squares are turned inside out and pressed. Stitch neatly to close the gap.

2 • Fold the corners to the center and fasten temporarily with one or two stitches. Whipstitch the four squares together on the back.

The Secret Garden units are all the same size—about 1½ inches (4 cm) square. Each one has been hand appliquéd to the background. Careful positioning was necessary to maintain the radiating lines as more units were added with each successive ring.

Asymmetry was introduced by offsetting the center of the radiating circle of units. Each unit had to be carefully positioned as they were stitched onto the background to achieve this effect.

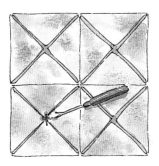
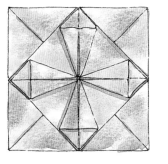

3 • Release the stitches fastening the corners to the centers.

4 • Refold the flaps to create folded patterns. Fasten points down by hand or machine. The squares could be further embellished with buttons or embroidery.

5 • Different patterns can be created depending on how you refold the flaps.

Stitching to a background

By working directly with the fabrics on a design wall, Sara decided to abandon the usual grid format for Cathedral Window, and developed the idea of stitching the units to a background rather than stitching them together.

DREAMING IN COLOUR

"I trained originally as a painter, and in more recent times studied patchwork and quilting, progressing from traditional techniques to using textiles as a vehicle to express my ideas. Initially these are developed from sketches, paintings, and collages in my notebooks. This provides me with color combinations and design possibilities, but often the quilts are as much about less tangible concepts like emotions and dreams. Some of my work combines unlikely influences, for instance lyrics of Bob Dylan songs with the work of artist Friedrich Hundertwasser. This quilt is one of an ongoing series inspired by the work of this painter."

LINDA KEMSHALL

This richly textured, abstract composition features a mixture of techniques and media. Machine appliqué, free-motion machine quilting, hand-stitched embellishment, beading, and foiling are all integrated. Materials include cotton, silk, and tiny beads. Linda first created the surface design by dyeing the basic cotton and silk fabrics. Tiny reflective beads and a combination of free-motion machine quilting and random hand stitching added further texture. The scattered shapes reflect the artist's internal themes, and a dreamlike quality is created by the repeated receding shapes.

Inspiration

The architectural work of artist Friedrich Hundertwasser inspired a whole series of quilts, which includes *Dreaming in Colour*.

Overall design

The quilt is composed of four rectangles of varying sizes, each one a complete image in itself but linked by echoing shapes, some of which stray across the dividing spaces. Flashes of yellow and reflective foil enliven the somber color palette.

Reverse appliqué

Foil was placed behind the areas to be worked in reverse appliqué, then the spirals were cut away to reveal it. Further embellishment was added using a satin stitch.

FOILING

1 • Using fabric glue or fusible web, create a design on fabric. If using glue, wait for it to dry before proceeding to step 2.

2 • Place the iron-on foil—a thin layer of metallic plastic attached to cellophane—over the design, colored side up. Cover the design with a cloth, and press with an iron.

3 • Lift the foil at a corner to check that the metallic color has transferred to the design. The fabric can be hand washed, but not dry cleaned.

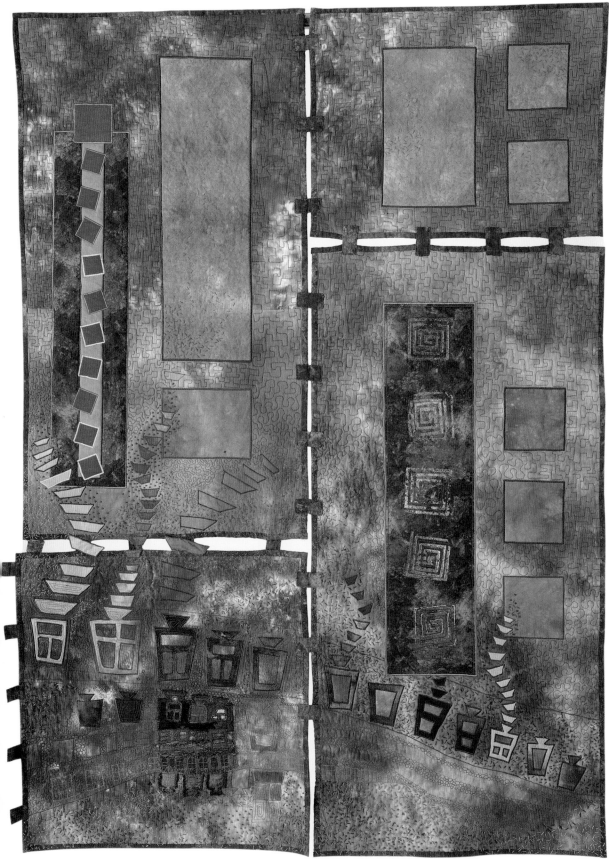

Machine appliqué using fusible web
Shapes were bonded to the background, then machine appliquéd using a close satin stitch in brightly colored threads.

Surface embellishment
Seeding (see page 26) was worked over large areas of the surface with a thick thread. This was combined with free-motion machine quilting to provide a variety of textures.

Size: 39 x 76 inches (100 x 193 cm)

INDIGO SQUARES

"I wanted a simple design to show off a variety of fabric-manipulation techniques using my own indigo hand-dyed fabrics, so what could be more basic than a Nine Patch. I worked out the scale and proportion on squared paper, as the border had to work in with the center Nine Patch. Within the basic Nine Patch each of the patches is divided again into smaller squares."

EDWINA MACKINNON

Fabric manipulation encompasses a variety of techniques that change the surface of fabric and create texture. There are traditional techniques such as Cathedral Window, in which the surface of the fabric is altered with folding, stitching, and the addition of contrasting fabric, and Yo Yos, in which gathered circles of fabric are whip-stitched together to produce an open-work fabric. Contemporary quiltmakers have developed new ways of manipulating fabric, inspired by crafts as diverse as origami and weaving. Working in a palette of soft blues, Edwina put three innovative techniques together in a simple Nine Patch format. The symmetry of the squares is balanced by the different textures and the subtle color changes in the indigo fabrics. The different techniques all work together to add an intriguing dimension to the traditional Nine Patch, giving this quilt a strong tactile, as well as visual, appeal.

Overall design

Fabric manipulation transforms a traditional pattern—the Nine Patch—into a contemporary quilt. On a larger scale, the border repeats the origami techniques used in the center patch.

Inspiration

Origami—the art of folding paper into decorative patterns—provides a source of inspiration for quilters experimenting with fabric manipulation techniques.

Origami techniques

Many of the folding techniques used in origami can be translated to fabric. One form of origami, sometimes called J.R. squares, is used in the center square and borders of the quilt.

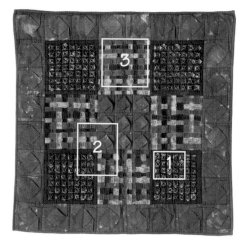

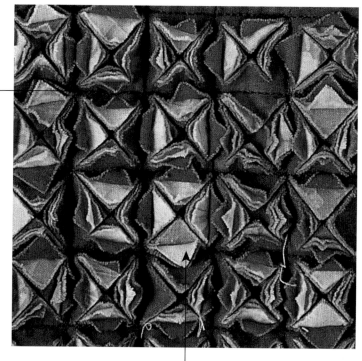

Subtle variations in the hand-dyed colors of the stacked fabrics are revealed when the layers are cut and frayed.

Within the Nine Patch formula there is a wealth of textural detail. The play of light and shadow on the folded panels and the rough textures of the frayed and woven edges of the fabrics are examined in more detail.

Fabrics were stacked, stitched in a grid, and cut to create a fluffy texture known as blooming.

Detail 2: Quilting

Because of the heavily textured nature of the quilt top, machine quilting was kept to a minimum. Edwina did just enough quilting to hold the layers together. A low loft cotton batting was used so as not to add more bulk to the quilt top.

BLOOMING

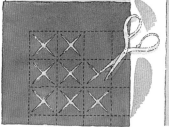

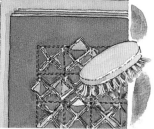

1 • Stack four layers of identical-sized fabric squares, right sides up. Press the stack with a hot iron. Mark a grid of horizontal and vertical lines ¾ inch (2 cm) apart on the top fabric, leaving a ½ inch (1.5 cm) margin all around the edges. Stitch along all lines on the grid.

2 • Using embroidery scissors or a small rotary cutter, cut through all the fabric layers, making crossed diagonal lines across each small square and taking care not to cut through the lines of stitching.

3 • Smooth the panel over another square of fabric, pin, then stitch over the grid lines. Brush the cut edges with a dry nailbrush to release the layers and increase texture, or run the piece through a washing machine and dryer for a fluffier finish.

TORN WOVEN STRIPS

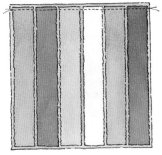

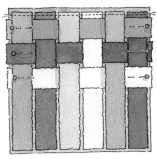

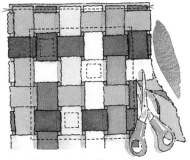

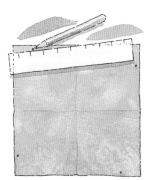

1 • Place torn strips of fabric ¾ inch (2 cm) wide in vertical lines across a backing square. Machine stitch along the top to secure.

2 • Weave strips horizontally across the square, pinning at each end to secure. Allow for the outside strips becoming absorbed into the seam allowance—a panel of nine by nine strips will finish to seven by seven visible strips.

3 • When the backing square is covered, stitch ¼ inch (0.75 cm) away from the outer edge of each second strip in, as shown. Where strips cross, add further stitching to secure. Trim ¼ inch (0.75 cm) from the stitching along each edge of the square.

1 • Fold a 6 inch (15 cm) square of fabric into a square. Press with an iron to crease and then unfold. Mark a dot 1 inch (2.5 cm) from the left-hand side of each corner as shown.

Detail 3: Fabric weaving

The background squares of fabric onto which the woven strips are attached should not be visible, so the colors of the fabric for the square and the strips were matched. Care was taken to butt together the edges of the strips as they were woven.

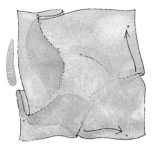

2 • On each side, bring the crease to the dot as shown, pleating the fabric, and pin in place.

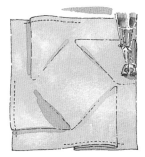

Strips of fabric are torn along the straight grain of the fabric. The edges of the strips are encouraged to fray, and then the strips are woven together.

3 • Tweak the center into a diamond shape and steam press. Stitch the pleats in place.

OUT OF THE DARKNESS

"Once I had learned the basics of quilting, I began to look at quilts to decide what it was that I liked about them. First, it seemed to be the colors and fabrics, but not the standard calico type that is more usual for patchwork. After a few color classes, it was not long before I was designing quilts of my own. I finally became secure enough in my own work to know that I could break the rules—using non-traditional types of fabric, machine quilting, and exploring new techniques. In the case of this quilt, I was coming out of a period of darkness. The gold moon slivers are bursting out in playful anticipation of the future."

BONNIE LYN MCCAFFERY

In her search for ways in which exotic fabrics could be incorporated into quilts, Bonnie developed a technique she calls "fantasy fabric." This technique involves layering materials—such as sheer fabrics, metallic lamés, decorative thread, Tintzl, and netting—and then stitching them together by quilting with invisible monofilament thread. Bonnie comments, "creating fantasy fabrics is fast and fun. Lots of pieces with beautiful curves are created easily without having to turn under all of the edges. I don't usually start out with a design or theme in mind, it's almost like the subconscious is at work delivering a message."

Overall design

Gold crescent moon shapes float across a nebulous background of varying tones and textures. Sheer teardrop shapes behind these create the darker areas that cross the surface diagonally. The quilting, in smoke-colored monofilament thread, provides an allover texture of swirling shapes that complement the design.

Construction technique

The techniques used in the construction of the quilt are a development of shadow appliqué—fabrics are trapped in the middle layer under sheer netting.

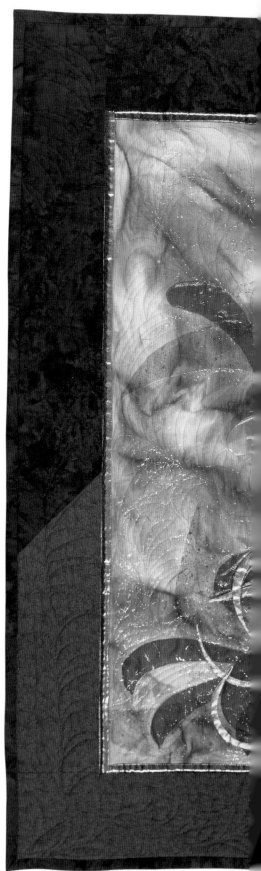

SIZE: 51 x 40 INCHES (130 x 102 CM)

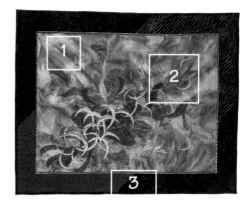

Details show how the quilt was constructed by using pieces of exotic fabric trapped between a hand-painted cotton background and a top layer of net, secured together by quilting.

Detail 1: Hand-painted background

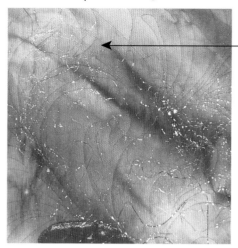

The background fabric is cotton, hand painted in colors—green through gray—that set off the shapes on the surface.

Detail 2: Quilting

The quilting forms a decorative texture and holds the layers in place. Free-motion quilting was stitched in a design that echoes the shapes, using invisible thread on the top and regular thread to match the back in the bobbin.

Crescent moon shapes in metallic gold fabric form a highlight of the abstract composition.

Detail 3: Border

Diagonal stripes on the border fabric reflect the direction on the main panel of the quilt.

LAYERING EXOTIC FABRICS TO CREATE A NEW SURFACE

 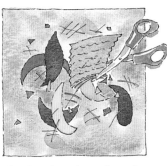  

1 • Place an ironed piece of cotton fabric (hand-dyed or painted fabric can be used) on a flat surface. Cut freehand shapes from decorative fabrics and arrange. Secure temporarily with pins or fabric glue.

2 • Cut tiny pieces from the fabrics and short lengths of thread and scatter them onto the surface in groups.

3 • Cut a piece of sheer organza or tulle netting the same size as the background and smooth over the composition, taking care not to snag it. Pin layers together using fine pins.

4 • Starting in the center, and using free-motion stitching and smoke-colored monofilament thread, quilt freehand over the surface, trapping the middle layer in place. For prominent quilting, use decorative thread.

Exotic fabrics

Look for decorative fabrics similar to those used by Bonnie in shops that supply fabric for theatrical costumes, Indian sari silks, and embroidery supplies. Search out metallics, lamés, and sheers to experiment with.

Color study

When selecting or creating a background for this type of work it is best to stay in harmony with the fabrics being used for the composition. Here, the muted colors and soft edges of the painted backdrop provide interest without dominating, and allow the shapes on the surface to stand out more.

The border is pieced from different fabrics, because Bonnie did not have enough of any one fabric to complete it entirely. Also, the sides of the border were longer than the standard fabric width. Her creative solution to these problems has led to an interesting result.

FOCUS ON FUNGI

"My quilts reflect the struggle between the natural environment and man's sustainable development. For some time I have been photographing various forms of fungi. Those that I photographed on a trip to the Bunya Mountains in Queensland, Australia were the inspiration to design and make Focus on Fungi. *The quilt was the first of a mini series on fungi."*

CYNTHIA MORGAN

Cynthia works intuitively with fabrics to convey a design idea, and her quilts evoke striking images of realism and life in the most minute detail. To create this piece, she first drew a small-scale design depicting the placement of the tree trunks and fungi panels. The positions of the fungi panels were outlined with tacking before the dye-painted background was machine quilted. The realism of the fungi panels was achieved by a number of strategies. Embroidery techniques were combined with hand dyeing and molding of the forms, and innovations such as singeing the edges of the leaves with a soldering iron were used to simulate decay. The separate elements were hand sewn and couched onto each fungi panel, then the panels were hand stitched in place. These textured images provide glimpses into a microscopic world magnified and highlighted on the forest floor.

Overall design

The forest floor, dye painted directly onto cotton fabric, forms the backdrop for five panels of magnified fungi. Lighter in color and on a heightened scale to the background, the finely observed and astonishingly realistic details provide remarkable focus areas.

The forest floor

Cynthia's artistic skills are apparent in the depiction of fallen leaves and forest floor litter, which set the scene for the fungi panels.

SIZE: 60¼ x 42¼ INCHES (153 x 107 CM)

Inspiration

Cynthia's interest in and involvement with the natural environment leads her to make photographic studies, from which she draws inspiration for her prize-winning quilts.

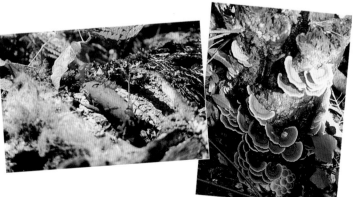

Each of the five panels displays Cynthia's dedication to every aspect of her work. The painting of the forest provides an atmospheric environment for the detailed fungi panels. From the initial dyeing of the fabric through all the stages of creation, her mastery of fiber art is in evidence.

Each of these panels reveals the minute observation, artistry, and skill that went into making the quilt. Cynthia says, "Through the age-old traditions of quilting, the individuality of different fibers has been explored in detail, and a new art form is emerging."

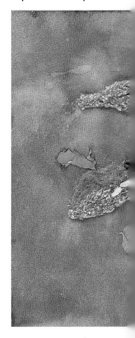

Cynthia painted directly onto the cotton background, referring to a small sketch that depicted the placement of the tree trunks and fungi panels.

Detail 3:
Top left-hand panel

Detail 1: Painting & stitching

Once the tree trunks and forest floor had been painted, machine quilting was stitched over the background, except in the area where the fungi panels were to be positioned.

The completed fungi panels were hand stitched in place on the quilt.

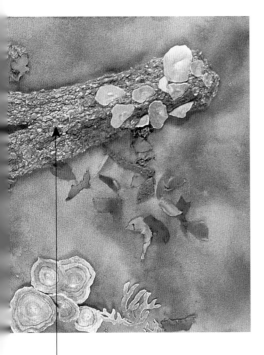

Scattered leaves, fungi, and a decaying, fallen branch are molded and sculpted using a combination of techniques—the logs were made by layering and embroidering dyed yarns onto a felt base; the leaves and fungi were constructed from hand-dyed and painted fabric.

CREATING THREE-DIMENSIONAL DETAILS

Leaves, shells, or other simple shapes can be made as separate elements to add extra dimension to a quilt's surface. You can use commercially available fabrics or hand dyes.

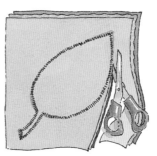

1 • Make a fabric "sandwich" by placing batting between two squares of fabric. The right sides of both fabrics should face outward. Draw a shape onto one side of the fabric, and machine stitch around the outline using straight stitch to fasten the layers together.

2 • Set the machine stitch to close satin stitch and, using decorative thread, zigzag around the outline of the shape, covering the straight stitches. Fasten threads and cut out the shape close to the stitching.

3 • Stitch the shapes to the quilt, attaching only part of each shape so that they will lift away. Shapes can be overlapped and the joining stitches can be used to add further detail.

SEDUCTION OF THE DAY

"Art surrounded me in my formative years—my mother was a strong influence, and my first experience with fiber was watching her embroider. Having been given the seeds of an art foundation at home, I went on to study interior design at college. I began quilting 13 years ago, after seeing a local quilt guild show. My first viewing of quilts sent me spinning in a whole new direction. It was at that pivotal moment when something inside me changed; I had a life-changing experience. I knew that quilting was what I had to do."

DIANA SWIM WESSEL

Overall design

Set in a background of organic swirling shapes, a large flower image fills one corner—it has a female form with wings flowing from it—symbolizing the need for freedom to travel and fly toward dreams. A soft color palette of blended pinks and blue-greens enhances the theme.

Like many contemporary quilters, Diana approached quiltmaking from an art background. Discovering quilting expanded her artistic horizons into the media of fabric and thread, adding tactile and textural elements to her creative expressions. This piece was made for a client who loves orchids and exotic birds. By sketching many design variations, Diana brought the quilt design to life. The first step in making the quilt was to outline the main design features in black, free-motion stitching. Then, the image was formed using watercolor pencils and crayon. Appliqué techniques were used to layer in more colors and positioned to create high and low contrast areas. The result is a combination of pictorial imagery and symbolism, which effectively merges the medium of quilting with that of expressive art.

Quilting

Blue thread was used for the machine quilting and created a strong, linear design. In some areas it was also used to block in shapes in a manner reminiscent of pencil drawing.

SIZE: 24 X 30 INCHES (61 X 76 CM)

The fluid quilting stitches used in the main section of the quilt continue into the border, softening the frame.

Detail 1: Mixed media approach

Selected areas show in detail elements of the quilt that display various working methods. A number of media are combined with machine stitchery in the creation of this lyrical work. The hand-dyed base is further colored with fabric crayons and stitched to create an image.

Diana achieves the desired effect with her quilts by using a mixed media approach. She adds surface design to cotton fabric by hand dyeing and drawing directly onto it with oil pastels. Stitches act as an outline to define the images.

Detail 2: Free-motion or drop feed quilting

Free-motion or drop feed quilting is stitched by dropping the feed dogs on the machine and using the darning foot. This prevents the machine from moving the fabric under the foot, canceling the stitch length setting. This means that the quilter has to move the fabric by hand as the stitches are formed.

Detail 3: Leaf shapes

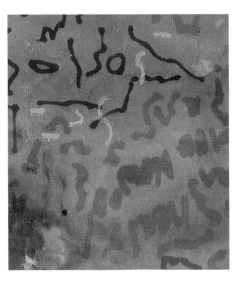

Solid leaf shapes are used in some areas, balanced throughout the quilt. These provide a contrast to the fluid, linear elements of the design created by the stitching.

Color study

Diana's mother, Jeanette Sciara, is a batik artist and has always been a major influence on her daughter's work. An example of Jeanette's batik fabrics is shown here. Batik is a form of resist dyeing: areas of fabric are painted with wax before they are dyed. The wax prevents the dye from coloring these areas. The wax is removed, fresh wax applied to other areas of the fabric, and it is dyed again—building up a number of colors.

APPLYING COLOR AND DESIGN TO FABRIC WITH OIL PAINTSTICKS

Oil paintsticks can be used on fabric to make a variety of marks and patterns. A mixture of linseed oil, wax, and pigment, they are available in a wide range of colors and can be fixed by heat setting with an iron.

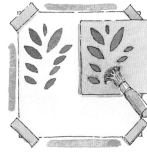

Color blending
Apply colors to the fabric surface, overlapping different colors. Blend with a rag dampened with a solvent such as white spirit.

Stenciling
Rub the paintstick onto a palette to deposit the amount of paint required, then use a stencil brush to pick up the paint and brush through the stencil.

Mark-making
Simple patterns can be worked directly onto the fabric with paintsticks. Secure the fabric to a flat surface with masking tape, then draw with the paintsticks.

THE ARTISTS

ANJA TOWNROW was born in The Netherlands, but came to live in England in 1977. Anja began making patchwork when pregnant with her first child, and carried on creating bedspreads in splendid isolation for ten years before discovering the world of quilting. She began exhibiting in 1995 and has since won several prizes. She also teaches and lectures on quilting.

ANN FAHL, the prize-winning quilter from Racine, Wisconsin, has exhibited pieces in solo and invitational shows in the United States, France, and Japan. She also lectures and gives workshops in the U.S.A. Many of her quilts and articles can be found in quilting publications worldwide, and she has recently released a CD-Rom, *The Quilts of Ann Fahl*. You can visit Ann's gallery on the internet at www.execpc.com/~fahl/index.html

BONNIE LYN McCAFFERY lives in northeastern Pennsylvania, and is the author of *Fantasy Fabrics: Techniques for Layered Surface Design*. Her other specialties include foundation-pieced kaleidoscope quilts and dimensional quilts. Bonnie loves traveling and teaching far and wide as it allows her to meet quilters from all over the world. You can see some of her quilts on her website at http:home.ptd.net/~bmccaffe or you can contact her by e-mail at bmccaffe@ptd.net

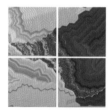

BRIDGET INGRAM-BARTHOLOMÄUS has lived in Germany since 1969, and in Berlin since 1981. She teaches patchwork, quilting, and embroidery internationally. Bridget became a member of Quilt Art in 1991, and has exhibited in numerous exhibitions.

CAROL SCHEPPS lives in Princeton Junction, New Jersey. She studied fashion and graphic design at Pratt Institute, Brooklyn, New York, and finds art quilts the natural medium for her artistic voice. Her work has been exhibited and sold in galleries, shows, and public places including *VISIONS 1998* and the University of Pennsylvania Hospital.
E-mail: cschepps@home.com

CAROLINE WILKINSON lives in London, England. She first became interested in quilting while living in the U.S.A. from 1979 to 1981. On returning to Britain she developed her skills with a local quilt group. She has since exhibited in national shows in England and Europe. She has co-authored a book on mini quilts and compiled quotes for *Quilt Note Book*. Caroline also teaches quilting in an adult education environment and to prison inmates.

CARYL BRYER FALLERT lives near Chicago, Illinois. She is internationally recognized for her luminous, award-winning art quilts, which have appeared in hundreds of exhibitions, collections, and publications throughout the world. Caryl travels extensively as a teacher and lecturer. To learn more, visit her website at www.bryerpatch.com

CHARLOTTE YDE lives and works in Copenhagen, Denmark. She originally trained as an embroidery teacher but has been producing quilts since 1978. Her quilts have been exhibited all over Europe, the U.S.A., and Japan, and she won the first prize in the European Triennial in Heidelberg in 2000. She teaches quilting and related workshops and has written five books and translated numerous others. You can learn more about her work by visiting her website at www.yde.dk, or e-mail her at charlotte@yde.dk

CYNTHIA MORGAN lives at Caloundra, on the Sunshine Coast of Queensland, Australia. Her prize-winning quilts are widely exhibited around the world, and are in numerous collections. She teaches internationally, and her book *A Quilter's Journey* was published in 1995 by Kangaroo Press. For more information e-mail cynthia@seq.net.au or visit her website at www.cynthiamorgandyequilts.com

DIANA BUNNELL of Boulder, Colorado made her first quilt in 1978, and has since attended many classes with famous quilt tutors. Diana's aim is to simplify the technical challenges of quilting and to find more spontaneous ways of expressing herself in fabric; she uses her quilts as a means of self-expression.

DIANA SWIM WESSEL lives in an old farmhouse in western Wisconsin, surrounded by her five children. After training as an interior designer, she began quilting in 1986 after attending a quilting show. Diana initially studied traditional designs and techniques before beginning to translate her own ideas into fabric. She has gone on to win many awards in national shows.

DILYS FRONKS has been making quilts for 16 years, learning and developing by using traditional methods. Through teaching quiltmaking, she has discovered an ability to be creative and this has encouraged her to be original in her approach and adventurous in her methods. She teaches locally in Wales and, as a member of the Quilters' Guild of the British Isles and the American Quilter's Society, has taught nationally and internationally. She has written three books on appliqué and is a regular contributor to quilting magazines. Her main interest is in appliqué and reverse appliqué using a needle-turn method and a table-top technique.
E-mail: dilys.fronks@talk21.com

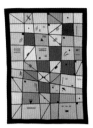

DIXIE HAYWOOD lives in Pensacola, Florida and has been quilting for over 30 years. Many of her quilts have won awards, and all have given her immense pleasure in their making. She is the author of over 160 articles and six books, four co-written with Jane Hall.
E-mail: roberthaywood@sprintmail.com

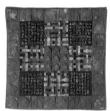

EDWINA MACKINNON of Worcestershire, England pursues her love of patchwork and quilting by not only creating wonderful pieces, but also by inspiring others through a variety of talks and workshops. Currently, her work is influenced by her own space-dyed and indigo-dyed fabrics, and she loves to explore the many ways of developing decorated, textured surfaces.

ERIKA CARTER lives in Bellevue, Washington with her husband and two children. She combines her sewing skills and innate color sense to create self-expressive quilts and over the years has produced more than 200 art quilts, and has received many awards for her work. Erika is also a founding member of the Contemporary Quilt Art Association, a group dedicated to furthering the acceptance of quilt as fine art.

FRIEDERIKE KOHLHAUßEN lives in Bad Homburg, Germany. She started quiltmaking in 1980, while she was living in the United States. Her work has been shown in numerous exhibitions around the globe and she has written three books on the art of quiltmaking. Friederike has taught and organized summer quilting workshops for many years, and in her role as President of Association Quiltkunst her aim is to promote the "art quilt" in Germany.

GABRIELLE SWAIN of Watauga, Texas is best known for her use of color and her craftsmanship. She began quiltmaking in 1983, and in her work, which ranges from realistic to abstract, she explores man and his relationship to nature. The author of two books on appliqué, Gabrielle has been featured in many publications, both national and international. She has also exhibited her work at many venues, and is one of the founding members of North Texas Quilt Artists. She maintains a working studio in her home, which she shares with her husband and son.

GINNY ECKLEY lives in Houston, Texas. She began creating with cloth at age 12. In 1995, she wrote *Quilted Sea Tapestries*, which specialized in machine embroidery techniques. Ginny teaches quilt and art classes and exhibits her artwork throughout the world. You can visit her website at www.fabricpainting.com or e-mail her at arthread@vonl.com

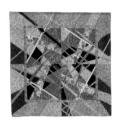

HILARY RICHARDSON lives on the south coast of England near Chichester. After initially training and working as a scientist, she now makes domestic and commemorative pottery and has been quiltmaking since 1987. Her work tends to be experimental, as she prefers to use fabric that she has dyed or treated herself. She lectures on patchwork and quilting and teaches workshops. She is also the International Representative of the Quilters' Guild of the British Isles 1998-2001.
E-mail: hilary.richardson@virgin.net

HIROMITSU TAKANO lives in Tokyo, Japan, where he teaches art to adults. Hiromitsu has authored books on honiton lace and sashiko quilting, as well as having work published in the Japanese quilt magazine, *Patchwork Quilt Tushin*. He has taught many different aspects of Japanese art all over Japan and the U.K.

INGE HUEBER lives in Cologne, Germany. She has been a full-time quilter since 1980. Inge is a founding member of Quilt Art, a European group of professional quiltmakers based in England. She exhibits and lectures worldwide.
E-mail: Inge.Hueber@NetCologne.de

IRENE MACWILLIAM lives in Northern Ireland, and has been involved in textiles for 15 years. She has exhibited all over the world, and teaches and gives lectures on both embroidery and quilts. Irene also belongs to a number of groups, including Fibre 2000, which consists of fiber artists from both the North and South of Ireland. E-mail: irene@macwilliam.force9.co.uk.

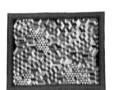

JANE HARDY MILLER lives in Miami, Florida. She has sewn all her life, and began designing and making quilts in 1969. The artist teaches patchwork and exhibits her prize-winning work at home and abroad.

JANE LLOYD of Ballymena, Northern Ireland has worked with fabrics for over 25 years. She exhibits locally, as well as in Europe and America, which she loves as it allows her to travel and meet like-minded people.

JENNI DOBSON of Loughborough, England has taught quilt-making since the late 1970s both nationally and internationally. Her work has been exhibited in America, Japan, Europe, and Australia. Author of several quilting books and many articles, she also edits a regular column in the magazine of the Quilters' Guild of the British Isles. Please visit her website for further information or to contact her: www.dobson4qu.freeserve.co.uk

JO WALTERS lives in Miami, Florida. She began making award-winning quilts in 1988. She teaches her signature BigStitch technique in workshops and through publications. She can be contacted by e-mail at jgw2@yahoo.com

JOAN COLVIN is noted for her use of the subdued colors of the northwestern United States, where she lives on Puget Sound. She has written books and taught and lectured internationally. Her work has been shown in solo, invitational, and juried exhibitions, and can be seen in numerous private collections in the United States and Europe. E-mail: colvin@valleyint.com

JUDY B. DALES of Kingwood, Texas has been quilting since 1970, and is best known for a distinctive, unique color sense and quilts with curved-seam piecing. Her work is included in collections worldwide, including a piece included in *The Twentieth Century's 100 Best American Quilts*. Her book, *Curves In Motion* showcases many quilts and presents techniques and designs for curved-seam piecing. E-mail: JUBDA@aol.com or visit Judy's website at www.members.aol.com/JUBDA/

JUDY MATHIESON lives just north of San Francisco in Sebastopol, California. She has been making quilts since l973. She has taught quiltmaking across the U.S.A. as well as in Canada, Japan, Australia, and the U.K. Her work has been exhibited widely and she has written two books about Mariner's Compass quilt designs. Examples of Judy's work can be seen on her website at www.members.aol.com/judy4quilt

KATHARINE GUERRIER of Worcestershire, England has been producing quilts and embroideries for over 20 years. She studied at art school and taught for some years before dedicating her time to quilting and teaching patchwork and embroidery. Her work in quiltmaking is quite varied and draws upon both traditional and contemporary influences. This book is one of several that she has written on quilting and patchworks.

KATIE PASQUINI MASOPUST has traveled all over the world teaching contemporary quilt design. Her style has developed over the years through traditional, to mandalas, then dimensional quilts, and now she is experimenting with landscapes. She has won numerous prizes and exhibits her work both nationally and internationally.

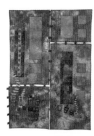

LINDA KEMSHALL lives and works on the Staffordshire/Shropshire borders in central England. She exhibits and lectures in Europe and North America and her first book was published by Martingale & Co. in 2000. Find examples of her quilts on the internet at www.kemshall.freeserve.co.uk

MARGARET DAVIDSON lives near Wolverhampton, England. She taught herself quilting in the 1970s and has never looked back. She has combined her passions for Art Deco, Modern Architecture, Amish quilts, and the quilting stitch itself to develop her own style—strong geometric shapes in solid fabrics.

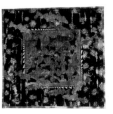

MARTA AMUNDSON lives on a small cattle ranch with her husband Larry near Riverton, Wyoming. She has been making quilts about endangered animals and the environment since 1989. Marta exhibits internationally and has taught in the U.K., Sweden, Brazil, Australia, and the U.S.A. Marta writes for quilting magazines in addition to a monthly column for the Front Range Contemporary Quilter's newsletter. Visit her website at www.homestead.com/amundsonquiltmaker/amundsonquiltmaker.html or e-mail her at marta-amundson@wyoming.com

MARY MAYNE lives in Bedfordshire, England. Her interest in patchwork and quilting began in the 1960s. She has won many awards, and shares her knowledge through teaching and lecturing. Some of her work is held in private collections, and she has also had two solo exhibitions.

MAURINE NOBLE of Seattle, Washington State has been developing and teaching machine quilting and machine appliqué since 1987. She has authored two books, *Machine Quilting Made Easy* and *Basic Quiltmaking Techniques for Machine Appliqué*, and co-authored *Machine Quilting with Decorative Threads*. E-mail: emnoble@televar.com

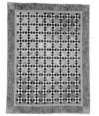

NANCY S. BRELAND lives in New Jersey. Her quilts appear in juried shows in America, and pictures of them are frequently published in *Quilter's Newsletter* and in other magazines and books. When she is not quilting, she works as a psychology professor at The College of New Jersey. E-mail: nbreland@tcnj.edu

PAM WINSEN lives in Brisbane, Australia. She has been making quilts since 1988. She has been awarded many prizes and has exhibited her quilts in Japan, the United States, and Europe as well as Australia. Her present work is cutting edge, combining oil painting with fabric, thread, and timber.

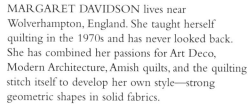

PAULA NADELSTERN lives in New York City. She is the author of *Kaleidoscopes & Quilts*, and she travels extensively throughout the U.S.A. teaching her unique kaleidoscopic quiltmaking techniques. Her award-winning quilts have been featured internationally in exhibits, television shows, books, and magazines. Paula's quilt *KALEIDOSCOPIC XVI: More is More*, was chosen for the prestigious book and exhibit *The Twentieth Century's 100 Best American Quilts*.

REBECCA COLLINS lives in St. Asaph, Wales, and has been producing quilts since 1986. Her prize-winning work has been widely exhibited; she teaches quilting courses and workshops and has inspired many of her students to become prizewinners themselves. She has written for both patchwork and quilting magazines and books. E-mail: rebecca@dermaguard.co.uk

ROBERTA HORTON lives in Berkeley, California. A quiltmaker since 1970, she began teaching in 1972 and has since taught and lectured in 12 countries. She was named as one of the 88 most influential quiltmakers in the world by Nihon Vogue, publisher of *Quilts Japan*. She was the recipient of the Silver Star Award for 2000 from the Houston Quilt Festival.

ROSEMARY PENFOLD has lived all her adult life in Brisbane, Australia. Given a needle and thread at the age of four, she has a life-long love of sewing and fabrics. She started patchwork in 1983 and has been teaching for ten years. She has exhibited nationally and internationally, and her first solo exhibition is planned for October, 2000.
E-mail: russellandrosemary@bigpond.com

RUTH B. MCDOWELL of Winchester, Massachusetts began quiltmaking in 1972, and has since become a full-time professional quilt artist, with over 300 quilts and five books to her credit. Her quilts intertwine the themes of nature and geometry with the piecing medium and an abiding love of fabrics.

SANDIE LUSH lives near Bristol, England with her young family for whom she started making quilts in 1990. Inspired by the legendary Amy Emms, she has specialized in making wholecloth quilts since 1994. These have been widely exhibited, winning many awards. E-mail: Sandielush@quilts.freeserve.co.uk

SANDY BONSIB lives near Seattle, Washington State with her husband, two teenagers, and many animals, all of which have provided subject matter for her quilts. She has been a quilter since the early 1970s. As a profesionally trained teacher, Sandy lectures and teaches at quilt retreats, quilt shops, and quilt guilds. She is currently writing her fourth book about quiltmaking. E-mail: sjbonsib@aol.com

SARA IMPEY lives in Earls Colne, Essex, England. She made her first quilt while still at school in 1971. Her background is newspaper journalism, but she has been quiltmaking seriously since the early 1990s. Her prize-winning work has been widely exhibited in the U.K. and internationally. She lectures on and writes for magazines about patchwork.
E-mail: robin.impey@lineone.net

SHEENA NORQUAY lives in Inverness, Scotland. She started doing patchwork and quilting in the mid 1970s, but she also works full time as a primary school teacher. She exhibits her work locally and nationally, and has recently started showing abroad. She uses her teaching skills to give day workshops and lectures about quilting and patchwork during the school vacations.

SHEILA YALE lives in Beckenham, Kent, England. She has been making patchwork since the days when she was a student at the Royal College of Art. Her motivation in quilting is to preserve beautiful printed fabrics and to bring them to the attention of others.

VALERIE HEARDER left her homeland of South Africa in 1975 and currently lives in Newfoundland, Canada. Well known for her miniature landscapes, she wrote a book on this topic, *Beyond the Horizon*. Valerie's work is in both private and corporate collections, she teaches internationally, and her work has appeared in numerous publications.
E-mail: val@nf.sympatico.ca

WENDY LUGG lives in Perth, Western Australia. A trained artist, Wendy works from a home studio, balancing precious studio time with ever-increasing travel commitments to exhibit and teach internationally. Her awards include a Churchill Fellowship and a Quilters' Guild Scholarship. Examples of her work can be seen on her website at www.wendylugg.com
E-mail: wendy@wendylugg.com

INDEX

CREDITS

The author would like to thank the following for their contribution toward the production of this book:

All the quilters for agreeing to participate by generously lending their work and providing background information.

My husband, **George Hudson** for his unfailing support in this and other publications.

Christine Porter for advice and assistance in contacting contributors.

June Morris for her expertise and advice on fabrics.

Kate Michell and **Sally Bond** for their constructive advice, and **Carrie Hill** for interpreting my diagrams into artwork.

Quarto would like to thank and acknowledge the following for supplying pictures reproduced in this book:

(Key: t = top, b = bottom, l = left, r = right, c = center)

p14c courtesy of Rebecca Collins, p24b courtesy of Wendy Lugg, p34 Pictures Colour Library, p40 courtesy of Caryl Bryer Fallert, p60tl courtesy of Katie Pasquini Masopust, p70tr courtesy of Sandy Bonsib, p.71 courtesy of Martingale & Company, p79c courtesy of Jenni Dobson, p84t courtesy of Maurine Noble, p90b courtesy of Pam Winsen, p100t Harry Smith Collection, p124 courtesy of Martingale & Company, p130br courtesy of Inge Hueber, p132t Pictor, p136tl Moira Clinch, p147b courtesy of Cynthia Morgan, p153tr courtesy of Diana Swim Wessel

All other photographs and illustrations are the copyright of Quarto. While every effort has been made to credit contributors, Quarto would like to apologize should there have been any omissions or errors.